Reinventing Government?
Appraising
The National Performance Review

Donald F. Kettl

La Follette Institute of Public Affairs
University of Wisconsin-Madison

Center for Public Management
The Brookings Institution

August 1994

Center for Public Management
The Brookings Institution

CPM Report 94-2

Based on Part One of
Inside the Reinvention Machine: Appraising Governmental Reform
(forthcoming from The Brookings Institution, Winter 1994)

JK
469
1994c

Copyright © 1994
The Brookings Institution
1775 Massachusetts Avenue
Washington, DC 20036

Contents

Foreword	iii
About This Report	iv
Executive Summary	v
Introduction	1
1. Tensions: Which NPR?	5
The Three-Front Revolution	5
Delivering the Savings	7
Improving Performance	11
Summary	12
2. Capacity: What Will It Take to Do the Job?	13
Public Employee Unions	13
Managers and Management	16
Solving the Quiet Crisis	18
Summary	20
3. Ideas: What Are the Guiding Principles?	22
Continuities	23
Discontinuities	25
Assessing the Critics	26
Summary	29
4. Glue: How to Hold the Movement Together?	31
The New Puzzle of the Public Interest	31
Customer Service	33
Performance Management	40
Summary	45
5. Missing Pieces	47
Civil Service	47
Investment	47
Steering	48
Congress	49
High-Risk Programs	51
Learning	52

Summary	53
Conclusion	54
Notes	63
Appendix I	76

Foreword

As we near the first anniversary of Vice President Gore's <u>Creating A Government That Works Better & Costs Less: A Report of the National Performance Review</u>, the debate over governmental reform has moved from the arena of rhetoric to that of implementation. And it is here that it will face its biggest challenge — creating meaningful, sustainable administrative change.

This report of the Brookings Center for Public Management does not trace progress on each of the recommendations made by the Vice President's report. Rather, it steps back and examines the reform efforts with both a scholarly and historical eye, and identifies the strengths of the effort, as well as obstacles to its lasting success.

This report is a product of the Brookings Center for Public Management. The views expressed in this report are those of the author and should not be ascribed to the trustees, officers, or other staff members of the Brookings Institution.

Bruce K. MacLaury
President

August 1994
Washington, D.C.

About This Report

This report is a product of the Brookings Center for Public Management. It is an interim product of a larger project that has closely examined governmental reform efforts under Vice President Gore's National Performance Review since September 1993. An edited volume based on this work, Inside the Reinvention Machine: Appraising Governmental Reform, will be published by Brookings this winter. Contributing to the project are:

Editors: John J. DiIulio, Jr., professor of politics and public affairs, Princeton University, and director, Brookings Center for Public Management; and Donald F. Kettl, professor of public affairs and political science, La Follette Institute of Public Affairs, University of Wisconsin-Madison, and visiting fellow, Brookings Institution.

Authors: Carolyn Ban, associate professor, Nelson A. Rockefeller College of Public Affairs, State University of New York; Christopher H. Foreman, senior fellow, Brookings Institution; Gerald J. Garvey, professor of politics, Princeton University; and Beryl Radin, professor, Nelson A. Rockefeller College of Public Affairs, State University of New York.

Supporting Publication: John J. DiIulio, Jr., Donald F. Kettl, and Gerald J. Garvey, Improving Government Performance: An Owner's Manual (Brookings, 1993).

Executive Summary

Vice President Al Gore's National Performance Review (NPR), with a report issued in September 1993, promised nothing less than a revolutionary reinvention of the federal government. Critics dismissed it as hollow rhetoric, and some scholars criticized it as dangerous. In its first year, however, the NPR has produced impressive results: a genuine start on changing the culture of government; simplification of some rules and procedures, especially by eliminating the onerous *Federal Personnel Manual* and the much-hated SF-171 job application form; a reform of the procurement process; improved top-level coordination of the government's management; and the stimulation of widespread innovation by federal managers through "reinvention labs."

The NPR produced more than almost anyone, including perhaps the reinventers themselves, believed possible. Even when the movement produced sketchy results, the problems it attacked usually were the right ones. However, to get the NPR moving, the reinventers made short-term tactical decisions to get quick wins. *The quick wins, though, have come at the cost of building the foundation for lasting success. As a result, the NPR is not now self-sustaining.* It has shown great potential, but the risk is that the NPR will become just a short-term political tactic instead of a lasting reform.

Two problems, in particular, have plagued the NPR.

1. A preoccupation with savings over performance improvement. Of course, a government that works better *can* cost less, as the NPR report's subtitle suggests. Streamlining procurement can save money, while a more customer-focused government can tailor programs more carefully to citizens' needs. In practice, however, seeking big savings in short order can undermine the broader effort for management improvement and increase costs in the long run. The largest single chunk of the NPR's promised $108 billion savings was to come from downsizing the federal work force ($40.4 billion). The downsizing was to be the product of the NPR's management improvements. The Clinton administration's eagerness for quick savings, however, led officials to shrink employment first and let the management improvements follow.

On one level, the focus on budget savings quickly alienated many government workers. The NPR had built a strong pro-bureaucrat case. It told public employees that the government's performance problems were the fault of the system, not of its workers. It also held out the promise of much greater flexibility for managers ("empowerment") and a reduction in red tape. The prospect of reducing federal employment by 272,900 workers, however, quickly preoccupied many managers and soon became the defining reality of the NPR for many government workers.

On another level, the savings proved far easier to promise than to deliver. The administration has had recurring disputes with members of Congress and the Congressional Budget Office about the savings from individual proposals. These disputes diminished congressional support for the NPR and delayed pieces of the legislative program, especially the bill that provided buyout payments to employees who agreed to leave the federal service.

Moreover, the savings proved the hardest element of the NPR to judge. Some long-term savings required short-term investments, like the buyouts. Some short-term savings risked increasing long-term costs, especially if downsizing in the absence of a "reinvented" workplace led the wrong employees to leave or weakened government management. Putting hard numbers on the NPR's savings, other than counting federal workers who left the government, required extraordinary feats of budgetary analysis. That complexity not only increased the difficulty of assessing the NPR's savings but also sometimes surrounded the NPR with debate of such technical detail as to undermine their political value. In the meantime, the downsizing led many bureaucrats not to enlist in the NPR's revolution, but to hope that it would soon go away. And since the public assumes that the NPR has long since produced the promised savings, the reinventers face the task of living up to the pledge as the task of achieving it — without undermining the rest of the movement — becomes ever greater.

2. The lack of an explicit strategy for dealing with Congress. NPR officials initially believed that they could accomplish most of their reforms without seeking congressional approval. The lesson of the first year, however, is that virtually no reform that really matters can be achieved without at least implicit congressional support. The NPR has not yet developed a full strategy for winning that support.

Congress embraced the broad downsizing initiative and, in fact, increased the reduction from 252,000 to 272,900 employees. For months, however, members stalled the buyout bill required to produce the savings, in part because of uncertainty about whether it would cost or save money in the short run. The House, meanwhile, voted to exempt the Veterans' Health Administration, with 212,000 employees, from the downsizing, so as not to threaten veterans' health care. The Senate then voted to exempt federal criminal justice activities, so as not to jeopardize the war on crime. Many members of Congress supported the NPR in the whole, but then tugged at its individual threads in ways that threatened to unravel it.

At the beginning, the NPR had concentrated on launching its report. It had not developed a strategy for implementing its recommendations beyond trying to enlist legions of bureaucrats throughout the agencies in the cause and hoping that the power of the ideas would defuse opposition. Members of Congress had everything to gain from embracing the broad principles of reinvention and then protecting their constituents and favorite programs behind the scenes in committee rooms and little-noticed riders to complex bills.

For the NPR to endure, it will need to build congressional support. That will require striking a different kind of bargain between the executive and Congress. The NPR's recommendations need congressional support; Congress needs a strategy for meaningful oversight. Although this requires an uneasy balance, both the president and Congress have a strong interest in shaping it. The stakes for the executive branch, both political and managerial, are clear. Moreover, especially in Congress's Governmental Affairs and Government Operations Committees, there is fresh interest in defining a new congressional role in management. Without finding a new kind of bargain between the branches, it would be easy for the congressional micro-politics of the NPR to nibble away its key elements.

In sum: The NPR, in its first year, accomplished far more than cynics suggested might be possible. It has launched a broad reform movement in the right direction, and it has been asking the right questions. Nevertheless, and this is the NPR's critical problem, *the short-term accommodations it made to get the movement going weakened its chances for long-term success.* It is not now a self-sustaining revolution, and considerable work needs to be done to move the invasion from a beachhead to a breakout, and then from a breakout to a conquest. Launching the reinvention revolution was the easy part. Sustaining the revolution will require much harder, and far less glamorous work. It will require considerable creativity, far more than either the reinventers or their critics have demonstrated, in recognizing and solving the four critical underlying problems that lie beyond the beachhead.

First, *tensions*: There really is no such thing as *the* NPR. It has, in fact, been a three-front campaign: to shrink the size and cost of the government; to spread a new gospel of reinvention in areas like procurement reform and customer service; and to encourage an army of reinventers throughout the federal government. However, NPR's outside game, based on shrinking the government, undercut its efforts to transform the government's inner workers because it alienated many public employees. Long-term success requires the NPR to ensure that, on each of its fronts, its strategies complement and do not disrupt each other.

Second, *capacity*: The NPR report argued the need to bulldoze away overbearing forces of supervision, authority, and oversight. The report, however, was far weaker on what ought to spring up in their place. The overwhelming lesson of the last generation of policy experimentation in the United States is that government programs do not manage themselves. Rather, success depends on finding the institutions, processes, money, technology, and especially people — that is, the capacity — to do the job. Will a reinvented government transform itself into a leaner government, faster on its feet and better able to adapt to the dizzying pace of change? Or will the legacy of reinvention be an even more hollow government with far less capacity to do its job, a government managed by employees with even less incentive to do their jobs well? The former would produce a truly revolutionary change. The latter would worsen the cycle of raised expectations, disappointing results, increased inefficiency, and greater public cynicism. Long-term success requires the NPR not only to explain what it wants to sweep away but, more important, to define what ought to spring up in the place of dysfunctional systems. Strengthening government capacity will require more than adherence to the broad themes of employee empowerment and customer service.

Third, *ideas*: The NPR built on ambitious ideas about cutting red tape, putting customers first, empowering employees, and cutting back to basics. Far less clear, however, was what the concepts actually meant. Where do procedural due process and proper administrative safeguards become red tape? Who are the government's customers and how can they be served? Does customer service contradict other public goals? What would it take to empower employees, and what risks would empowerment create? Who decides what the basics are? In their best-selling book *Reinventing Government*, a driving spirit of the NPR, David Osborne and Ted Gaebler make the case that government should "steer, not row." But in what direction should government steer, and how good are the ideas that serve as its compass? The lessons from reinventions abroad and private sector reform in the United States is that a clear sense of purpose and sharp guiding principles are critical to success. Long-term success requires the NPR to define, far more sharply, its purpose and guiding principles, if it is to escape the quicksand of fuzzy rhetoric.

Finally, *glue*: The NPR builds on a philosophy of "empowering" government workers to make better decisions. It argues for a more "entrepreneurial" philosophy, with a competition prescription replacing monopoly-based command-and-control management. In short, the NPR seeks to shift power from Congress to the bureaucracy and, within the bureaucracy, from top to bottom levels. If empowered bureaucrats behave entrepreneurially, what glue will prevent government from disintegrating into a vast network of quasi-independent operators? What processes will ensure democratic accountability to elected officials? What processes will ensure that the public interest dominates private behavior? Long-term success requires the NPR to build a force at the center of government, perhaps in the Office of Management and Budget, to focus government on results and avoid having the reform spin off into scores of different, unconnected directions. It also requires the NPR to focus sharply on striking a new kind of bargain with Congress over government management.

Even more fundamentally, achieving the NPR's promise will require more clearly linking the question of *what* government ought to do with *how* government ought to do it. The NPR, in the report's own words, "focused primarily on *how* government should work, not on *what* it should do." The burden of a century of public management research, however, is that the distinction is artificial: the how powerfully shapes the what because means embody ends; from the beginning, the how has to be driven by the what.

To a greater degree than even political noncombatants stop to recognize, and certainly far more than government officials ever acknowledge, many public performance problems are the product of what government sets out to do. Government in fact does many things very well, from delivering social security checks to providing weather satellite maps. Often, when things work badly, it is because government tries to do things that are very hard or impossible, like preventing drug abuse, training unemployed workers, cleaning up toxic waste, or providing welfare without creating dependence.

Improving performance on one level requires focusing government most clearly on the things it does well and figuring out how to do them better. However, we (and this includes the NPR, policymakers, and Americans in general) have not thought clearly about what those things are. On another level, if we seek to do things that are hard to do well, we must be frank about the degree of difficulty and focus sharply on how to do the impossible better. Many of the most basic questions to which the NPR has addressed itself revolve around such issues. If we choose to attack these problems at a superficial level, by focusing on the number of bureaucrats that can be eliminated or the dollars that can be saved, we will both miss the real issues and even further undercut government's ability to perform well.

The National Performance Review accomplished, in just its first year, far more than anyone thought possible. It energized employees, it attracted citizens, it drew media attention to government management, and it made the point that management matters. In the blush of success, however, the NPR failed to build the foundation for success in the long haul. It borrowed bits and pieces of management reform from both the public and private sectors and pasted them together in a patchwork that, while initially attractive, could not hold together. In the process, the NPR missed the most important lesson that other successful reforms teach: in the long run, management, matched to mission, matters most. The movement launched in September 1993, however promising, was not self-sustaining. Making it stick requires hard work on tough questions — work that, for the most part, has not begun.

Introduction

When Vice President Al Gore released his National Performance Review (NPR) report in September 1993, some cynics dismissed it as just another hollow piece of rhetoric. Academic critics attacked it as dangerous to the public interest. They were wrong. In its first year, the NPR has proven one of the most lively management reforms in American history. It has helped reorient the federal bureaucracy toward a far more effective attack on problems that it must learn to solve. Public support has been overwhelming.

Indeed, a careful review of the NPR's first year shows impressive results that disprove the cynics:[1]

- *A quick start on culture change.* The report's theme that government had to work better and cost less resonated profoundly. Measuring the precise impact of the report on the culture of government agencies is impossible, and making such an ambitious change stick will take a generation. But one conclusion is already certain: After the report, neither the behavior of government workers nor the debate about their jobs can ever be the same. The NPR's four key principles — cutting red tape, putting customers first, empowering employees to get results, and cutting back to basics — provided new, if rough, guideposts by which to steer and judge the federal bureaucracy.

- *Simplification of rules and processes.* The NPR has also helped disentangle some of the rules and procedures that hinder effective federal management. In particular, the Office of Management and Budget (OMB) has issued waivers to make it easier for agency officials trying to survey citizen satisfaction with public services.[2] The Office of Personnel Management (OPM) eliminated the huge *Federal Personnel Manual* and the government's monstrous all-in-one application form, SF-171, in delegating personnel decisions to government agencies.

- *A reform of the procurement process.* The Clinton administration's enthusiastic support and hard work dovetailed with ongoing congressional effort on procurement reform. The result is an important simplification of the procurement process — the first major reform of the government's contracting rules and procedures in a decade.[3]

- *Improved coordination of the government's management activities.* The NPR recommended designating a "chief operating officer" within each cabinet department to oversee management and to promote culture change. In addition, the NPR suggested that the chief operating officers comprise, together with a handful of other top officials, a "President's Management Council" (PMC) "to lead the quality revolution and ensure the implementation" of the NPR.[4] In just a few months, the PMC has proven not only a valuable weapon in the Clinton administration's efforts to marshall support in the agencies for the NPR. It has also proven an important mechanism for focusing government-wide attention on key management issues and for organizing political support for major legislative issues. The coordinated efforts of PMC members contributed greatly to the passage of the first piece of the NPR legislative program.[5] The PMC also provided a secluded forum in which top officials could compare approaches — a "counsel council," in the words of Alice Rivlin, who chaired the PMC as OMB deputy director before being named the office's director.

- *Widespread innovation by federal managers.* The NPR encouraged agency heads to establish "reinvention labs," and more than one hundred sprang up throughout the government.[6] While there is no systematic survey of what these labs have accomplished, mounting evidence suggests that these reinvention labs represent exciting innovations in the federal government. Not all of the labs are likely to produce successes; the whole point of experimentation is to find what works and what does not. But the labs are generating a mountain of fresh ideas and information about how government workers can do their jobs better.

Vice President Gore has recognized "heroes of reinvention" around the government who had helped slash government red tape. One hero, the Department of the Interior's Roger Patterson, cut the process of approving fish ladders over dams from two and a half years to six months, and from thirteen steps to just eight. The old process, Patterson said, "wasted a lot of time. It wasted a lot of money, and it wasted a lot of fish." Rodney Martin, a Small Business Administration employee in Texas, introduced a simple loan application for small business operators that replaced a far larger form. Meanwhile, General Services Administration (GSA) officials replaced long approval forms, which cost $50 each to process, with a new credit card for routine purchases.[7]

The NPR has unquestionably generated an enormous amount of activity, enthusiasm, and positive effort. Not all of the initial results can be traced directly to the NPR. Indeed, some of the earliest successes came from experiments started during the Bush administration. The NPR, however, unquestionably accelerated the pace of change and provided political cover for managers trying to break out of hide-bound routines. Most important, the NPR generated a fresh sense of the possible. Managers were amazed that ideas that had lain fallow for years suddenly sprang to life. Small but important reforms that top managers had previously dismissed suddenly received higher-level approval.[8] The frenzy of activity did not convince all of the cynics, especially long-time mid-level government workers who had watched waves of reform wash over the bureaucracy for years without effect. But the NPR unquestionably fueled new excitement and energy.

The first year of the NPR has generated more progress than almost anyone — indeed, perhaps more than the reinventers themselves — imagined possible. To get the NPR moving, the reinventers understandably made short-term tactical decisions to get quick wins. *The quick wins, however, have come at the cost of building the foundation for lasting success. As a result, the NPR is not now sustainable.* Indeed, some of the tactical decisions made to get the movement under way have undercut the chances for building in the long run a government that works better and costs less.[9] This does not mean that the NPR is destined to fail. But the ultimate fate of the NPR will depend on the reinventers' success solving four critical problems.

First, *tensions*: The NPR has played an outside game, focused on downsizing the federal government, and an inside game, focused on transforming the government's culture. At the most basic level, both interconnect in the effort to improve government's performance. After all, the subtitle of the NPR report promised "a government that works better and costs less." Some of the movement's biggest headlines, in fact, came from the pledge to produce $108 billion in savings, especially by reducing the number of government employees and transforming the procurement process. At the operational level, however, it was natural for government employees to see the downsizing as yet another explicit attack on their jobs and behavior. NPR's strategy for public support — shrinking the federal government — risks undercutting its efforts to transform the government's inner workings by alienating public employees.

Second, *capacity*: The NPR was dominated by arguments about dysfunctional forces, about processes and structures that interfered with performance. Indeed, there was considerable suspicion within the NPR about supervision, authority, and oversight. The report argued the need to bulldoze away these forces. The report, however, was far weaker on what ought to spring up in their place. The overwhelming lesson of the last generation of policy experimentation in the United States is that government programs do not manage themselves. Rather, success depends on finding the institutions, processes, money, technology, and especially people — that is, the capacity — to do the job. Will a reinvented government transform itself into a leaner government, faster on its feet and better able to adapt to the dizzying pace of change? Or will the legacy of reinvention be an even more hollow government with far less capacity to do its job and managed by employees with even less incentive to do their jobs well? The former would produce a truly revolutionary change. The latter would worsen the cycle of raised expectations, disappointing results, increased inefficiency, and greater public cynicism.[10]

Third, *ideas*: The NPR built on ambitious ideas about cutting red tape, putting customers first, empowering employees, and cutting back to basics. Far less clear, however, was what the concepts actually meant. Where do procedural due process and proper administrative safeguards become red tape? Who are the government's customers and how can they be served? Does customer service contradict other public goals? What would it take to empower employees, and what risks would empowerment create? Who decides what the basics are? In *Reinventing Government*, a driving spirit of the NPR, David Osborne and Ted Gaebler make the case that government should "steer, not row."[11] In what direction should government steer, and how good are the ideas that serve as its compass? Fuzzy thinking could staff the oars with government employees rowing simultaneously in conflicting directions. The lessons from reinventions abroad is that a clear sense of purpose and sharp guiding principles are critical to success. Is the NPR intellectually mature enough to define such a purpose and provide guiding principles?

Finally, *glue*: The NPR builds on a philosophy of "empowering" government workers to make better decisions. It argues for a more "entrepreneurial" philosophy, with a competition prescription replacing monopoly-based command-and-control management. In short, the NPR seeks to shift power from Congress to the bureaucracy and, within the bureaucracy, from top to bottom levels. If empowered bureaucrats behave entrepreneurially, what glue will prevent government from disintegrating into a vast network of quasi-independent operators? What processes will ensure democratic accountability to elected officials? What processes will ensure that the public interest dominates private behavior?

The NPR has the potential, together with the New Deal and the Hoover Commissions, to be one of the three most important administrative initiatives of the twentieth century.[12] Moreover, the NPR has demonstrated several important things. The public constituency for bureaucratic reform proved far larger than anyone anticipated. Many public managers, as eager as anyone to make government work better, proved quick embraced the opportunities the NPR presented. Positive results, in the form of both lower costs and improved performance, are palpable. Most important, however, the tough knots tangling the work of the federal government and the jobs of federal executives have proven far tougher to cut than the initial waves of enthusiasm suggested.

Having established a beachhead, the NPR invasion cannot be allowed to fail. The stakes, in the public's trust in its government and government's own ability to adapt to ever-growing demands in an era of tight resources, are huge. Launching the revolution was the easy part. Sustaining the revolution will require much harder, and far less glamorous, work.[13] It will require considerable creativity, far more than either they or their critics have demonstrated, in recognizing and solving the critical underlying problems that lie beyond the beachhead.

1. Tensions: Which NPR?

Assessing the NPR is difficult — there is no such thing as *the* NPR. In practice, the NPR has been a messy and sometimes disorganized multi-front war against the government's performance problems.

The Three-Front Revolution

There are, in fact, three different NPRs. First, the NPR's supreme commanders, especially senior staff members working out of the vice president's office, have focused on how the NPR can help the Clinton administration attract voters. The administration's political strategists have worried constantly about how to win the approximately 19 percent of American voters who supported Ross Perot in 1992. They have focused single-mindedly on the NPR's cost savings and personnel reductions as critical elements in the Clinton administration's reelection strategy.

Second, the NPR's skeletal staff has concentrated on preaching the gospel of reinvention to anyone who would listen and on coordinating the crosscutting reform issues, like procurement reform and customer service. The NPR has relied heavily on Presidential Management Interns and staff from government agencies on short-term detail to the effort. There has been only a small continuous core to the NPR staff, and that has limited its ability to ensure consistent follow-through.

Third, an army of reinventers throughout the executive branch has had primary responsibility for most NPR efforts. Nearly all of the 384 recommendations in the NPR report, in fact, relied on actions by individual agencies.[14] For example, the report charged NASA with improving its procurement practices, the Department of Labor with creating one-stop career management centers, and the Environmental Protection Agency with supporting market-based instead of regulatory approaches to pollution control. Agency-based commanders carried the reinvention flag into the bureaucratic trenches, to apply the movement's broad principles to their agency's specific problems.

Because it has operated simultaneously at such different levels and pursued such varied objectives, it is difficult to assess fully the NPR's results. Indeed, the revolution has proceeded on many different fronts, and the fighting has mattered as much as the winning. In part, this was because the movement's leaders believed that front-line bureaucrats were the best judge of the right direction. In part, this was also because they believed that inertia posed the greatest problem. Forcing innovative action was the quickest way, in their minds, to ensure success, and activity became NPR's immediate measure of success. The NPR's six-month status report was little more than a study of motion (laws passed, executive orders issued, action started).[15]

Assessing the NPR's more fundamental results is difficult because it has pursued radically different, indeed conflicting, goals. The NPR seeks, in the words of its subtitle, a government that "works better and costs less." On one level, of course, more effective programs can save money. On a deeper level, however, the subtitle represents an uneasy truce between opposing camps in the reinvention effort. During the Clinton administration's six-month performance review in 1993, the "costs less" forces, led especially by political strategists within the White House, argued that nothing mattered as much as shrinking the size of the government. The "works better" team, championed by followers of *Reinventing Government* (including Osborne himself) and hundreds of government workers detailed from federal agencies, argued for changing the culture of federal agencies to improve public programs. The tension between them was resolved during the fiscal year 1994 budget battle, in August 1993, when the struggle over the last few votes in the Senate led administration strategists to pledge that the NPR would produce extra savings to reduce the budget deficit. The $108 billion in savings promised by the NPR soon became the bedrock of the movement.

As a result, the ghost of deficit reduction lurked behind every promise of empowering workers or improving performance. The short-term payoff from the tactic was huge. Public support for the NPR report was overwhelming and delivered the Clinton administration the strongest bump in public support during its first eighteen months in office. Moving from the headlines to the front lines, however, surfaced the conflict implicit in the "works better/costs less" theme. Because the largest single piece of the promised savings was to come from reducing the number of federal employees, the threat to their jobs became the defining element of the NPR for most federal employees.

There was a major disconnect between the "works better" and "costs less" objectives. The NPR staff trumpeted "doing more with less." Government workers, however, believed that they had already been stretched to the limit by a decade of budget cuts; struggling to do their jobs with even less help could only mean doing less with less, they worried. The focus on using the NPR to produce cost savings risked both undercutting the government's capacity to do its work and bureaucrats' incentives for taking the considerable risks that the NPR demanded. Indeed, some government employees began calling the reinvention movement "reinvent-sham."

The disconnect between the two objectives of the NPR had an important tactical advantage for each. The downsizers could allow the performance improvers considerable latitude so long as the promised savings materialized. On the other hand, the preoccupation of the downsizers with the budget cuts gave the performance improvers considerable maneuvering room in charting fundamental change. Thus, in the first year, the disconnect gave the Clinton administration good headlines yet insulated the front lines from political interference.

This tactical advantage, however, hurt the movement's long-term potential. Actually producing the savings proved far more difficult than the report promised. And the search for quick deficit reductions undercut the long-term effort to improve government performance.

Delivering the Savings

Most of the $108 billion savings the NPR promised would come from three categories: reducing the size of the bureaucracy ($40.4 billion); program and organizational changes in individual agencies ($36.4 billion); and a 5 percent reduction in procurement costs by streamlining the contracting process ($22.5 billion).[16] The Clinton administration, in fact, quickly produced a major piece of legislation to deliver the first $6 billion of savings from fiscal years 1994-1998.[17]

Downsizing the bureaucracy by 252,000 (later 272,900) persons was the keystone of the cost savings.[18] Where did the magical 252,000 figure come from? Although many observers believed that the figure was an arbitrary one, Robert Stone, NPR project director, had an explanation:

> We made a head count government-wide of supervisors, budget specialists, financial specialists, personnel specialists and headquarters people, plus regional offices. The total count was — I think the report says 690,000. We have a little later count that's about 670,000. We said, "This is twice as big as it ought to be."
> But if you cut that group in half, you have to substitute for them — for example, groups that measure progress, that set goals. So you can't just cut 335,000. The judgment was that maybe a quarter of what you cut out you ought to put back to perform these other functions. So half of the control and micromanagement force is 335,000, a quarter of the 335,000 is 85,000 or 83,000. That leaves you at about 252,000. That's roughly the arithmetic.[19]

Stone and his NPR colleagues believed that government's problem lay with the layers of checkers and cross-checkers. By reducing those employees, they believed, the government would be leaner and more effective. About 55 percent of the cuts, moreover, were to come from the ranks of middle managers,[20] although neither the report nor subsequent discussion made clear exactly who was in the "middle."

Several problems plague that logic, however. First, the target came from an *assumption* about where and how large government's problem was, not the result of any careful analysis nor of an assessment of what kind of government was needed. There was no assurance, therefore, that the downsizing would shrink government in the right places.

Second, there was considerable risk that the downsizing plan would induce the wrong workers to leave first. Indeed, many of the officials who quickly took advantage of the buyout were some of the most seasoned managers — those who had the most opportunities in the private sector — in whom the government had for decades invested a great deal. The downsizing threatened to be indiscriminate, and government managers worried that they would lose some of their best people.[21]

Third, the NPR argued that the government's problem was its layers, not its people. In particular, the report argued that the federal government had far too many middle managers. As Paul Light has found, however, government's most significant layering problem occurs at the very top, not in the middle. The 3,000 political appointees that populate the top of the bureaucracy can produce layers upon layers of officials between the president and the career service.[22] Attacking the middle would do nothing about the problems at the top. The debate soon became moot, though, as the incessant downsizing pressure made the NPRers preoccupied with the numbers instead of the layers.

Fourth and most important, the targets quickly became the political acid test of the NPR. Strategic planning initially was to drive the cuts, but the head-count game quickly replaced the planning. The downsizing target became the administration's most politically visible target, and hence its most vulnerable front. By committing itself to an arbitrary reduction, the NPR eliminated any chance that a serious look at the composition of the work force and the skill mix of government would drive the reductions. The downsizing became the political pass/fail test for the NPR.

There was a widespread assumption that the downsizing would be imposed across the board. In fact, during the first full year of the personnel cuts (fiscal year 1995), two-thirds of the reduction was to come from the Defense Department, as part of the broader reduction in the defense establishment. Some other agencies were to be held even while others were to achieve relatively small reductions. Neither was the downsizing uniform across the levels of the bureaucracy or between Washington and field offices. That made it all the more difficult for the administration to describe clearly what the downsizing would accomplish and where it would occur (which, of course, only increased the anxiety of even the government workers who in the end would not be affected). Moreover, having harvested strong public support in the polls simply by *announcing* the reduction, administration officials were left with the tough job of doing the hard work of achieving it with little additional political capital to be won.

The savings, however, proved far easier to promise than to deliver. In October 1993, the administration packaged some of the reforms in H.R. 3400. Administration officials estimated that the bill would produce $6 billion in savings over five years.[23] The Congressional Budget Office reviewed the bill, however, and estimated that savings would total just 5 percent of that amount. In some cases, CBO argued that some of the administration's proposals (such as the work force reductions) would actually require near-term new spending (for incentive payments). In other cases (like improvement of Medicare claims processing), the administration had estimated savings that CBO did not believe would materialize. In yet other cases (like selling recyclable materials from defense installations), CBO found it could not confidently assess how much, if any savings, could safely be budgeted.

CBO's scorekeeping embarrassed the administration and undercut the confidence of many observers in the NPR's other savings estimates. Administration officials and members of Congress alike had looked hungrily at the promised $108 billion in savings as a funding source for new programs, like the administration's crime bill. If the savings proved hard to deliver, the enthusiasm of many policymakers would shrink. The dispute with CBO also caused the administration immediate trouble in winning congressional support for the buyout legislation, on which the downsizing and hence the largest piece of the NPR's deficit reduction depended.[24] Members of Congress were unwilling to pass the bill if they could not be confident whether it would, in the calculus of the deficit reduction process, save or cost money. In the end, OMB and CBO reconciled their disagreement over the savings in H.R. 3400, and the administration won passage of the buyout bill, but not before the dispute underlined three serious issues.

First, although the savings proposals were only a small part of the NPR, they became its driving theme. Cost reductions take up only a few pages (in the report's preface and in the department-by-department rundown in appendix A) out of 172 pages in the overall report. Nevertheless, because of the pressure on the administration to produce savings through the NPR and the administration's own efforts to sell the reform, the cost savings became the movement's political lightning rod. In the high politics of the NPR, nothing meant as much as the cost savings. This was, in part, because of the pressure on the administration to produce savings through the NPR and, in part, because of the administration's own efforts to sell the movement.

Second, amid all the rhetoric of "empowering employees" and "serving customers," the dollar savings seemed the most solid feature of the NPR. In practice, the savings proved perhaps the hardest element of the NPR to judge. Producing long-term savings sometimes required short-run costs, such as providing payments to government employees willing to leave the government. Sometimes short-term savings risked incurring long-term costs, if downsizing, for example, led the wrong employees to leave or weakened government management. In almost all cases, putting hard numbers on savings actually produced, beyond the downsizing of the federal work force, turned out to require extraordinary feats of budgetary analysis. That complexity not only increased the difficulty of assessing the NPR's savings but also sometimes surrounded the NPR with debates of such technical complexity as to undermine their political value.

Finally, Congress proved eager to support the savings proposals in general but often backed away from taking the actions in particular required to achieve them. In late April 1994, for example, the House voted to exempt the Veterans Health Administration (VHA) from any personnel reductions. The VHA accounted for 212,000 full-time employees, about 90 percent of all the staff at the Department of Veterans Affairs and larger than any other civilian agency. The Senate later voted to exempt federal criminal justice activities from personnel cuts. A few months later, when the Transportation Department submitted an NPR proposal to turn the nation's air traffic control system over to a government corporation, congressional opposition forced a hasty retreat. All three actions proved frightening omens for the reinventers' efforts to shrink federal employment.

Despite the support for the NPR that many members of Congress showed, they also demonstrated that they could easily unravel, strand by strand, its critical threads. As they were drafting their report, the NPR staff had devoted virtually no attention to building congressional support for their recommendations. They therefore had no offensive plan to build congressional support for the plan and no defense against forays against individual elements. When they first announced their report, NPR staffers argued that they could implement a majority of the recommendations without congressional action. The first year of their efforts demonstrated that they could launch and sustain *none* of the recommendations without at least congressional acquiescence. Even quick successes, like the creation of the National Partnership Council, connect eventually with Congress and its concerns about federal programs.

Table I

Department of Commerce "Permission Slip"

Ask yourself,

1. Is it right for my customers?
2. Is it legal and ethical?
3. Is it something I am willing to be accountable for?
4. Is it consistent with my agency's mission?
5. Am I using my time wisely?
6. Is the answer YES to all of those questions?
7. If so, don't ask permission. You already have it.
   JUST DO IT!

Improving Performance

On the front lines in the federal agencies, a quite different movement developed. The watchwords were *employee empowerment* to produce *culture change.* Commerce Secretary Ron Brown, for example, distributed "permission slips" to his employees (see table I) and Education Secretary Richard Riley issued "reinvention licenses." Secretary Brown's permission slips asked bureaucrats a series of questions. Is what I want to do right for my customers? Is it legal? Is it a wise use of my time? The permission slip then told employees that, if the answers are "yes," they already have permission and should press ahead. The presumption was that employees too often held back for fear of retribution; the solution is that empowered employees will take more initiative and solve problems more effectively.

Many federal employees, however, argued that such slogans were hollow and simple-minded. From previous reforms that had swept over government, they had learned two lessons. Bold rhetoric often had little substance behind it. And new revolutions soon replaced old ones, so they could easily wait out any new reform. Indeed, there had been total quality management, which replaced the Reagan administration's privatization initiatives, which followed on the heels of the Carter administration's reorganizations, which came after the Nixon administration's management by objectives, which succeeded the Johnson administration's planning programming budgeting system. "This, too, shall pass" was the watchword among countless managers (and "none too soon" others added under their breaths). Many managers had little confidence that reinventing government would produce any better results or prove any longer lasting than earlier initiatives.[25]

Not all federal managers wanted to be empowered, moreover. Being empowered meant taking risks, and the reinventers could offer little more than broad assurances that employees would not be punished if "empowered" behavior produced criticism. The impenetrable maze of forms and regulations, furthermore, worked to the great advantage of those who knew how to maneuver through them. One senior government official found that some senior bureaucrats had resisted the reinvention movement. "They have figured out how to maneuver within the current system," the official explained. "'Don't change it,' they say, 'because I've already figured out how to work within it.'"[26] Their power and comfort came from learning how to survive an admittedly dysfunctional system.

Finally, empowerment requires a top-down commitment to bottom-up decisionmaking. Many of the Clinton administration's top officials embraced the principle but were so overwhelmed by the demands of their offices that they had little time to promote it. "How do you tell political appointees who are already working fourteen hour days that they ought to be more committed?" one government employee asked.[27] As many lower-level officials worked on reinvention projects, they worried constantly about the degree to which they could commit their superiors to the process and, without their sustained commitment, how much real change they could effect.

"Empowerment" therefore remained a broad goal with shallow support. It was a heady concept only vaguely defined. It required new political leadership that was hard to produce under the press of regular business. It asked government employees to abandon an admittedly dysfunctional system, through which they nevertheless had learned to negotiate, for a far riskier way of doing business without any guarantee of compensating political support. Many government employees asked why they should take such risks when "empowerment" seemed only a rhetorical cover to threaten their jobs.

Summary

Reinvention throughout the federal government has proven a wildly uneven initiative.[28] In some departments, harried top managers paid almost no attention to reinventing government's goals. It seemed a distraction from what, to them, were far more important issues, and they followed only the letter of the presidential executive orders and directives. Other agency heads decided that reinventing their offices would have to wait until the endless appointments process produced a full complement of presidential appointees. On the other hand, some cabinet secretaries and agency heads saw in the NPR a license for broad managerial discretion. It allowed them to seize the reins of their agencies more quickly and to help sweep troublesome rules and processes, such as OMB clearances, out of the way.

However, for most federal managers, the defining reality of the NPR soon became the work force reduction. Despite the bold phrases in the NPR report about empowerment, customer service, reduction of red tape, creating market dynamics, forming labor-management partnerships, and investing in greater productivity, the immediate threat of fewer employees was what grabbed their attention.

The genius of the NPR lay in harnessing a wide variety of different ideas to build enthusiasm and launch some initial reforms. Its most fundamental problem, however, lay in moving from the first tentative steps to a broader movement that began to grow roots: in balancing the tensions created by contradictory ideas, and in providing managers a clear compass by which to chart their behavior.

2. Capacity: What Will It Take to Do the Job?

Stripped of the rhetoric and stories, improving government performance is fundamentally about people and the tools they need to do their jobs. In 1986, Charles H. Levine warned of a "quiet crisis" steadily but surely eroding the capacity of the federal government. Levine cautioned that the quiet crisis, "if left unattended, could produce major breakdowns in government performance in the future."[29] The Volcker Commission echoed Levine's concern and worried that, "if these trends continue, America will soon be left with a government of the mediocre, locked into careers of last resort or waiting for a chance to move on to other jobs."[30]

The evidence of America's performance problems might appear in ridiculous rules or tangled processes. Bulldozing through those rules and processes undoubtedly can help clear the way for real reform. But what will replace them? And more important, who will be there to do the job? After committing itself to sweeping away the detritus of a century of public management, after pledging employee empowerment and customer service, the NPR has not yet forcefully articulated a vision for the public service of the future. There is still time. Indeed, the NPR is preparing a civil service reform package for late 1994 or 1995. Without solving the people problems of American government, however, the NPR will be worse than incomplete. It will sow the seeds of its own undoing. Having dismantled an admittedly dysfunctional system without designing its replacement, it could leave public management even more impoverished and government performance even worse.

Public Employee Unions

The keystone of the NPR's people strategy lay in building bridges to public employee unions.[31] The NPR learned one lesson from its survey of private organizations: "No move to reorganize for quality can succeed without the full and equal participation of workers and their unions. Indeed, a unionized workplace can provide a leg up because forums already exist for labor and management exchange."[32] Building a partnership with the unions thus became the centerpiece of the NPR's relationship with government employees, and the core of union relations was to be a new National Partnership Council (NPC).

The NPC has a dozen members and is composed of the heads of the three major federal employee unions (the American Federation of Government Employees, the National Federation of Federal Employees, and the National Treasury Employees Union), the Public Employees Department of the AFL-CIO, representatives of seven federal agencies, and a special representative of the vice president. Its charge is broad:

> advising the President on labor-management relations; supporting the creation of labor-management partnerships and promoting partnership efforts; and proposing legislative changes related to labor relations, staffing, classification and compensation, and performance management . . . [33]

The NPC's importance lay both in the administration's desire to frame a new partnership with federal employees unions and short-term political imperatives. When the NPR became committed to a dollar target for cost savings, and when a reduction in the number of public employees became a prime vehicle for producing those savings, the NPR acquired an immediate political problem. For a Democratic administration already embroiled in controversy with the unions over NAFTA, another battle with unions was distinctly unappealing. The administration tackled the problem with a two-front effort: it devised a strategy of targeting the personnel cuts on middle managers, who tended to be less unionized than lower-level workers; and it promised union leaders the NPC as a forum for dealing directly with the administration.

The political strategy worked. The NPR avoided a quick counter-attack by the unions and in fact won their endorsement for the report. Moreover, the NPC got to work and helped lead the charge for abolishing the 10,000-page *Federal Personnel Manual*. In January 1994, Clinton administration officials and career civil servants joined together to throw the stacks of volumes into a dump truck parked outside the Office of Personnel Management (OPM). OPM Director James B. King, in celebrating the event, said, "It is written in such gobbledygook that it takes a team of Washington's finest attorneys to understand what is required to hire, fire, classify and reward employees . . . and that's nonsense."[34] Underlying the effort, however, was a harsh reality: The laws and regulations codified in the *Manual* remained in effect. If OPM was not going to use the *Manual* to transmit them, what would replace it? That question was unanswered and went to the heart of OPM's future role and the broader issues of personnel administration. If OPM was not to micromanage, what *would* it do? And if federal personnel laws, from equal employment opportunity to merit hiring regulations, were not to be centrally managed, *who* would manage them?

OPM continued to bulldoze away core elements of the existing system. Three months after abolishing the *Federal Personnel Manual*, OPM officials dumped the much-hated SF-171, the standard federal personnel application form. "I just think the ordinary citizen has no idea of how bad this form is," King said at the time. He demonstrated the fact by unfurling his own SF-171, which stretched to more than his own 6 foot, 4 inch height.[35]

These actions reflected serious ongoing talks within the NPR about four different issues:[36]

- bargaining on workplace issues, including empowerment; the rights of managers in hiring and disciplining employees; and compulsory union membership for government employees in units already composed of at least 60 percent union members;

- constructing an agency-based hiring process;

- collapsing the fifteen-level General Schedule classification system into a smaller number of so-called "broad bands"; and

- promoting performance management systems, including assessment of employees' work. Although such systems had been around for years, the NPR galvanized support for them. The discussion included streamlining the process for firing under-performing workers but was less clear on how under-performers would be identified.[37]

The NPC arrangement defused what could have been serious union opposition to the NPR. However, it also created difficult ongoing problems for the NPR. Representatives of government managers' associations, notably the Federal Executive Institute Alumni Association, the Federal Managers Association, and the Senior Executives Association, were furious that they had been excluded from the process.[38] These managers "were flabbergasted to hear of the creation of the NPC," said Allan Kam, a senior attorney in the National Highway Traffic Safety Administration and president of the Federal Executive Institute Alumni Association. "It was as though we were being disenfranchised."[39]

Representatives of nearly twenty different managers' groups organized their own committee to counter the NPC, the Coalition for Effective Change. The coalition began meeting regularly with NPR officials, but the administration's early deal with the unions coupled with the downsizing targeted at middle managers, unquestionably worsened the NPR's relations with many federal employees. Managers came to believe that the NPR was a two-track system, with different treatment for the unions and managers. In fact, they "were stunned that career managers, executives, and nonunion professionals had been excluded from the National Partnership Council."[40] The coalition made the point in its report to the NPR:

> The [NPC] Report . . . is silent on the role and treatment of managers and supervisors as *employees* in a changed system. Supervisors, managers, and management officials who are excluded from the

bargaining unit also are employees who have certain inherent rights to fairness and equity both individually and collectively that are not addressed in the Report. Who will speak for these employees . . . ? Who will represent their interests . . . ?[41]

Despite the central role that the public employee unions played in the NPR's first months, no one really knew how broadly the unions actually represented government workers. OPM statistics show that 59 percent of federal government employees (or about 1.3 million) work in units covered by bargaining agreements.[42] Only a relatively small fraction of employees in these units, however, are dues-paying union members, although the actual number is a secret closely guarded by the unions.

Union organization, moreover, varies tremendously across categories of federal employment. Nearly all (91 percent) of blue collar employees work in union shops, while only 53 percent of white collar employees are in units with exclusive bargaining agreements. On the other hand, three times more white collar than blue collar employees work in units with such exclusive agreements. Thus, although blue collar workers are more unionized, they represent a much smaller share of federal employment. The white collar unions are far more important. Union activity, however, varies widely across federal departments. In the Department of Housing and Urban Development, 77 percent of all employees are covered by union agreements; in the Department of Agriculture, the number is just 27 percent.[43]

That means a union-based strategy plays out very differently: by an employee's level (since lower-level employees tend to be far more unionized and top-level employees were excluded in the NPC); by kind of work (since white collar employees tend to be far less unionized); and by agency (since unions have been far more successful in organizing some agencies than others). The political advantages of the tactic are obvious, but the potential for building a long-term strategy for solving the quiet crisis of the civil service is far less.

Managers and Management

The NPR's tactics worried managers throughout government. Headlines of personnel newsletters ranged from "GORED!!! 'Reinventing Government' Plan Creates Spoils System"[44] to "From Rowing to Steering to Abandoning Ship."[45] The Federal Executive Institute Alumni Association surveyed a group of senior federal managers and found that 61 percent said that morale was low in their agencies, compared with 34 percent a year before.[46] "There are lots of angry SESers [members of the Senior Executive Service]," one federal manager explained. He was an administrator of a federal "reinvention laboratory," a strong reinvention advocate working the front lines of the reform. Nevertheless, he was discouraged by the downsizing campaign. Middle managers, he believed, were the targets of the campaign. "The middle chunk is a very disenfranchised group right now. They see little incentive to play because they weren't involved in framing the goals."[47]

Just who *are* middle managers? In the debate, the "middle" sometimes seemed to cover everyone just above front-line workers and just below political appointees. The NPR continually insisted that the cuts were addressed at the system, not the people. A memo from NPR staffer John Ayers to Robert Stone underlined that "the attack on the central control structures is not an attack on the employees."[48] Despite such assurances, however, virtually everyone who could potentially be considered a "middle manager" felt threatened by the NPR.

As the NPR evolved, the disconnect between the downsizing pressures and union partnerships and the strategy for improving government work and supervision grew wider. Managers — middle managers in particular — felt vulnerable and under attack just as they were being challenged to take more risks. Many middle managers laughed cynically at the NPR's charge to "do more with less," convinced that in the long run the only enduring legacy of the movement would be the cuts in government employment. In fact, many middle managers said that the defining reality for them of the NPR is the downsizing of the federal work force, and thus the threat to their jobs.

Middle managers play a critical role in the reinvention effort. They occupy the key positions throughout government that determine how well programs work. They are the project managers, branch chiefs, and section heads who shape programs and the behavior of their agencies. They model the behavior of their subordinates.

Vice President Gore has spoken enthusiastically about how a "shift of our understanding of human capacity" has led us to realize that "individuals within organizations are capable of producing more than had been previously thought possible." Revolutionary information technology has created the potential for flatter organizations with quicker response. Speaking to federal managers, Gore said, "[W]e can't achieve [major changes] by making a report. It can only be done by individuals. We are relying on you to lead this change."[49] Federal managers have heard the message, but the voice of large cuts in the government service has spoken even louder. Fulfilling the promise of the NPR depends on their action, but the NPR has singularly under-motivated them.

If the NPR is to have any real staying power, the movement will have to motivate the managers who most determine government's results. They have sensed the large disconnect between the symbolic appeal of downsizing the bureaucracy and reshaping the bureaucracies they are trying to manage. Some members of the career bureaucracy have quietly noted the irony that, although Ronald Reagan waged war on the bureaucracy, it remained largely unscathed by his presidency. Bill Clinton, on whom they had counted for support, produced the cuts that Reagan could never manage. Many federal managers worried out loud that enthusiasm for the "culture change" would evaporate, leaving behind only the residue of the cuts: a bureaucracy with even less capacity to tackle the challenges of a new century.[50]

Dealing with labor-management relations is not the same as dealing with supervisor-subordinate relations. The issues have through history always been different. In the context of the NPR, the distinction is even more critical. The report calls on managers to motivate their employees, to build broad partnerships, to cut across agency boundaries, to take chances. By building on a partnership with unions, the NPC approach reinforces much that helped create and maintain the very forces the NPR is seeking to change.

This is not to criticize the active role and significant accomplishments that the NPC has to its credit. Using such a partnership as the primary mechanism for dealing with the government's work force, however, carries grave risks for the NPR. It has alienated many government employees who are not union members. It especially has alienated government managers on whom partnership with the unions will ultimately depend. Most important, it has missed a chance to redefine the nature of government work and how the relationship among government workers ought to be transformed. It is a less-than-half-a-loaf solution that all too easily can lead reformers to convince themselves that they have in fact solved the problem.

Solving the Quiet Crisis

We know what needs to be done to create a high-performing civil service. Levine outlined the elements nearly a decade ago: strong political leadership; pay for performance; greater freedom for workers in entering and leaving the federal service; and a carefully designed pay scale to recruit and keep the best workers (an issue growing more important and more complex as increasing numbers of women and minorities join the federal work force).[51] We can add to that: greater freedom for managers in hiring, promoting, and firing workers (to which the NPR is committed); and constructing a system for measuring government performance (to which I will return in section 4).

More than anything else, however, we need an aggressively defined vision, bolstered by top-level support, of the new job of the federal executive.[52] In a March 1994 speech on "The New Job of the Federal Executive," Vice President Gore laid out seven principles to guide action (see table II). The speech was useful indeed. It was, however, more an outline for future thinking than a clearly developed set of principles.[53] Any set of principles has to take account of four important issues.[54]

1. Redefining the careers of civil servants. The existing civil service builds on a system of clearly defining administrative tasks and finding the best people to fill them. Both the rapid pace of change and the complexity of administrative demands has rendered that system obsolete. The modern civil service — indeed, all of American government — needs to be far lighter on its feet, quicker to adapt and change, and better equipped to deal with the challenges it faces. A reinvented civil service will have to invest more in people than process. People will have to be more mobile and faster to learn; agencies will have to acquire more flexibility to attract the people they need, if only on a temporary basis. Government employees will be working across organizational boundaries instead of being surrounded by them. In short, the American civil service must learn the lessons being taught around the world: the key reality is "the shift from a career service based on ongoing structural certainties to one based on agreed, ongoing values and principles" to compensate for rapid structural, procedural, and programmatic changes, as Denis Ives, the director of the Australian civil service put it.[55] The NPR must resist the temptation to replace the existing civil service procedures with new ones, when the problem is far deeper than just procedures. Macro-level values must drive the micro-level repairs.

2. Supporting public servants with technology. It is not unusual for college students to leave behind their campus computer labs for federal internships, only to complain when they return about the prehistoric technology they found. Over the last few years, the government has made great strides in better equipping federal managers with the technology they need to do their jobs. Nevertheless, managers lag behind their private sector colleagues in workplace tools. Managers, for example, are under heavy pressure to develop more customer-friendly processes, like single application forms for related programs. Federal workers often say that they would love to do just that, but they lack a computer system to link different offices and data bases together. The reinventing government initiative has largely been sold as a cost-cutting measure, and undoubtedly huge cost savings are possible. The truth, however, is that many long-term cost savings and increases in effectiveness will require up-front investment. The government cannot leapfrog into the 21st century with decades-old technology.

Table II

Vice President Gore's Vision of the New Role of the Government Executive

1. Developing a clear vision
2. Creating a team environment
3. Empowering employees
4. Putting customers first
5. Communicating with employees
6. Cutting red tape
7. Creating clear accountability

Source: Al Gore, "The New Job of the Federal Executive," Public Administration Review, vol. 54 (July/August 1994), pp. 317-31.

3. Training. One of the most important investments is in training. The NPR has recognized the importance of training government employees, especially to reinforce the messages of employee empowerment and culture change. The principal approach has been a method of cascading training: training the trainers, who in turn train others to spread the word.[56] While a valuable first step, it is not basis on which to institutionalize the NPR's goals. Making it stick over the long run will require a far larger investment in much more sophisticated training. Australia, by contrast, has been at government reform work far longer. Its public service invests 5 percent of the personnel budget in training and recognizes that failure to provide adequate training "may cause confusion about overall organizational aims and structure, with loss of motivation and decline in performance."[57] In the United States, by comparison, the federal government spends only 1.3 percent of its personnel budget on training.[58] Moreover, senior Australian officials have argued after reflection that it was the training they organized, especially for their middle managers, that proved most useful in their reforms.[59] Without far greater attention in the United States to training, and significantly more investment in the government employees who will daily do the job, the risk is that confusion, loss of motivation, and performance decline may indeed result.

4. Providing central steering. The NPR pledges to reform the personnel system by untying the central personnel rules and vesting more power in agency managers. Indeed, it has already moved a surprising degree in that direction. What, then, is the role of OPM if it gives away most of its work and authority?[60] The NPR suggests that OPM needs to transform itself into a consulting organization, "providing leadership for the cultural change."[61] That, to put it mildly, is not an easy process. It is not simple to change the internal culture of OPM from a regulatory agency into a consulting firm. Former regulators are not always good consultants, and in any case a new consulting agency ought to be far smaller than the old organization. But OPM's role needs to be more than advice giving. It needs to be the collector and analyzer of information on the two million workers in the federal service, tracking trends and forecasting future problems. It needs to oversee the newly empowered agency-based personnel systems, for a set of core values surely will remain. Most of all, OPM needs to set the tone, to transmit the values and principles that a reinvented work force will follow.

Summary

Despite warnings for years, the federal government is indeed in the midst of a quiet crisis. The NPR, in both its report and its subsequent actions, has recognized many of the roots. However, for short-term tactical reasons, the NPR's actions not only might not solve the crisis but might risk deepening it. There have been acts of commission, most notably entangling the government's downsizing with the pledge for employee empowerment and dealing with union but not management representatives. There also have been acts of omission. The resources devoted to training have been small, and the development of a new sense of the job of the federal executive is only embryonic.

The NPR nevertheless represents the best chance in a generation to attack government's performance problems and the quiet crisis that has helped produce them. But for the NPR to succeed, it must break through the cynicism that pervades government reform (and to which, in part, it has contributed). It is no secret, in Washington and around the country, that the federal government's civil servants are wary, cynical, and in some cases, even furious about the NPR.

Two overriding realities make things different this time around. First, the president and vice president have committed themselves, in an unusually public way, to the initiative. Congress has even enlisted in at least parts of the campaign. This reform has higher visibility, broader political support, and stronger legal backing than any other in a generation. Second, even though elements of the message might be fuzzy or even contradictory, the public is demanding higher performance and lower cost from government. The challenge for public management in the coming decade is developing new insights for improving performance as resources shrink but expectations rise. The public opinion polls, together with Ross Perot's 1992 presidential campaign, underline that the imperative is inescapable.

Government workers understandably are unhappy about the demands and uncertainties that swirl around them. Their jobs are being threatened, they are being asked to do more with less, they are being "empowered" to take more risks, they are told their performance will be measured far more closely. These are not easy steps to take, and a huge amount of uncertainty, complaint, and even attack is inevitable. But the reinventers in particular and government in general have little choice. A favorite slogan among the reinventers is "get on the train or get under it"; charting a course through high demands and inescapable conflicts is the only option, they quite rightly argue. If the problems are inescapable, so too are the anxieties of government workers. There is, quite simply, no easy way out and no way to avoid the turmoil.

Under such circumstances, it is hard to criticize the NPR for doing its best to balance tough political demands with broader managerial requirements. The reinventers have sailed as skillfully as any pilot could through these waters. Nevertheless, the undeniable fact is that the short-term bargains they made unquestionably have hurt their ability to fashion lasting long-term change. They have alienated many of the government workers, especially key managers, on whom they will need to rely to carry the flag into battle, and they have no clear strategy to get them back. Neither have they developed a strategy for building a fresh foundation for a strong and vibrant public service, upon which the future of reinvention will rest. Without solutions to both problems, the NPR risks even further deepening the quiet crisis of the civil service.

3. Ideas: What Are the Guiding Principles?

Vice President Gore and his staff launched the NPR with an overriding preference for action over ideas. They were far less worried about theory than about quick results. Nevertheless, important ideas were implicit within the movement they launched. These ideas, moreover, proved crucial in steering the movement. They defined the broad themes, communicated to government employees the kind of behavior the NPR desired, and helped shape the way the news media covered the NPR. The lesson of every major government reform around the world has been that ideas drive action — and frame the standards by which others judge that action. So taking stock of these ideas is critical in appraising the NPR.

For the NPR, two ideas were central. First, the reinventers argued, if implicitly, the need to transfer power from Congress to the executive branch. In the NPR report, Congress makes few appearances except as the source of overregulation and micromanagement, and those problems are critical to the NPR's diagnosis of government's performance problems. Reinventing government requires ending overregulation and micromanagement. That implicitly demands that Congress give up its penchant for tinkering with the bureaucracy and leave more of management to the managers.

Second, the Clinton reformers much more explicitly argued that government employees needed to be empowered. Real empowerment meant, in the jargon of private sector reformers, putting more decisions on the shop floor. In a production process, the ultimate symbol and reality of empowerment is the ability of any employee to stop the production line. That, in turn, demands that top managers decentralize power to front-line workers. The NPR builds on just that philosophy and envisions, both literally and figuratively, giving front-line government workers the power to stop the line. This approach is implicitly a philosophy of transferring power from Congress to the bureaucracy and, within the bureaucracy, from top-level to lower-level officials.

The reinventers built heavily on Osborne and Gaebler's *Reinventing Government,* earlier reform classics like *In Search of Excellence,*[62] and management gurus like Peter Drucker.[63] Newer ideas, from "continuous improvement" to "reengineering" crept into the reinvention lexicon as well, and private sector experience with these movements heavily flavored the early days of the NPR.[64] They also borrowed heavily on the lore of government reform abroad, especially in Great Britain, Australia, and New Zealand. The intellectual provenance was not always clear. In fact, the reinventers rarely stopped to make clear the intellectual provenance of their actions. They quickly culled through both private sector reform movements and government reforms abroad for ideas, any ideas, that promised some purchase on American governmental problems. As a result, they often seized on concepts that were complex, occasionally contradictory, often far beyond existing public management theory, and sometimes in advance of anything written down. That makes deducing the guiding principles of the NPR difficult, but it also makes it all the more important to outline and analyze them.

What mattered to the staff of the NPR was finding principles that could spark the movement, or notions that could fan the flames of reform. What they promoted has sparked many critics, especially among public administration scholars who contended that the movement was wrong-headed or even dangerous to American democracy.[65] In fact, the NPR builds on some time-tested administrative reforms. It also adds some ideas unique to American administrative reform. Together they constitute a surprisingly robust body of thinking with significant implications that sweep far beyond the NPR.

Continuities

Two important tensions from administrative history helped shape the NPR: the ageless battle between Hamiltonians and Madisonians over the proper role of executive power in American democracy; and the eternal debate within administrative theory over how to balance central control over policy with decentralized power to fit policy to particular problems.

On one level, the NPR is a recurring skirmish in a battle over executive power that has raged since the founding of the republic. Followers of Alexander Hamilton have long pressed for a stronger executive; long opposing them have been followers of James Madison, who argued for powerful democratic checks on executive power. Were Alexander Hamilton alive during the NPR's 1993 campaign, it would have been easy to see him as reinventer-in-chief. In the *Federalist Papers*, he argued for "energy in the Executive" and contended that

> A feeble Executive implies a feeble execution of the government. A feeble execution is but another phrase for bad execution; and a government ill executed, whatever it may be in theory, must be, in practice, a bad government.[66]

Hamilton believed that only a strong central government, led by a powerful executive, could help the country realize its potential.

Hamilton, of course, had a difficult time convincing most of his contemporaries, and in the end his strong views cost him his life in a duel with Aaron Burr. If the framers of the Constitution agreed on anything, it was that the mischiefs of the king's rule over the colonies would not be repeated. James Madison's genius lay in constructing a system which simultaneously recognized the inescapable need for an executive and constructed a system for holding executive power in check. The checks-and-balances system, in fact, is most fundamentally a strategy for checking and balancing *presidential* power. Congress was the first branch; its role was to assert the people's primacy, especially over the potential abuse of executive power.[67] If the judiciary was the least dangerous branch, the executive was the most dangerous one. True Madisonians, therefore, saw any attempt to increase executive power as dangerous.

The reinventers are Hamiltonians. Their views produced what Hamiltonian arguments always produce: strong, fierce reaction from Madisonians who quite predictably warned about the dangers of concentrated executive power. The attacks were strongest among many traditional public administration scholars who were, in their hearts, Madisonians, and who saw the NPR as a dangerous aberration from increasing and rightful congressional control of the executive branch.[68] The reinventers, meanwhile, reacted as Hamiltonians always do. They argued that a feeble executive threatened government performance, and that only more energetic, empowered bureaucrats could shrink government's performance deficit.

On another level, the NPR is about where power ought to rest over those decisions that policymakers put in the executive domain. This debate is even older than the Madison-Hamilton dispute and is, indeed, one of the ageless questions of administration, public or private. Centralization strengthens the hands of policymakers and their control over the actions of their subordinates. Such control, however, weakens the ability of front-line workers to match broad policy with the problems they find. Lower-level workers inevitably have at least some discretion. (Just how many drivers traveling over the speed limit should the highway patrol arrest — and how much speed over the limit warrants an arrest?) The centralization/decentralization issue frames an eternal dilemma: too much higher-level control limits the flexibility of lower-level workers to match broad policy with the special circumstances they find; too much flexibility by lower-level workers risks transforming the policy they are charged with administering into little more than the accumulation of ad hoc decisions.[69]

To argue for employee empowerment is also to argue for greater decentralization of decisionmaking. That, in turn, brings the NPR all the well-known risks of subversion of broad policy. The reinventers quite explicitly sought to take those risks, for they believed that excessive top-level control was choking innovation and undercutting performance. But in choosing sides, the reinventers quite predictably led critics to warn of the dangers that decentralization could produce: risks to equal protection and democratic accountability that centralized power could help avoid.[70]

Neither of the Hamiltonian-Madisonian nor centralization-decentralization disputes presents a sharp either-or choice. Indeed, the question is always how much executive power we wish to trade for democratic control, how much decentralized discretion we are willing to trade for less central policy control. But a reading of history produces two insights. First, critics from opposing camps howled about the dangers that a centralized, Hamiltonian approach presented. Like all strong arguments strongly put, the case for reinvention produced powerful reactions from the opposite poles. Second, the NPR, like every other reform ever tried, is inherently unstable. The arguments do not present an either-or choice but, rather, a range of options lying along a continuum. The heat of the criticism, however, sometimes obscured the choices. The forcefulness with which the NPR put forth its case, moreover, deflected attention from the important, enduring tradeoffs that the Hamiltonian-Madisonian, centralization-decentralization debates put sharply.

A careful look at the ideas underlying the NPR therefore helps explain its logic and the criticisms it has generated. It also charts the future challenges the NPR faces if it is not to become the problem to which future reformers seek fresh solutions.

Discontinuities

Beyond the continuities with previous reforms, however, the NPR built on a genuinely fresh notion that private-market incentives ought to drive public-sector performance. Ideas based in the "new economics" of organizations laid the foundation for this approach:

- *Contracts.* The key relationships in government can be viewed as a series of contract-like connections. While never explicitly acknowledged by the reinventers, this idea drives the innovative portion of the NPR.[71] It builds on interrelated theories that flow from formal economics. First, principal-agent theory holds that organizations can be understood as a series of relationships between principals (who have work to be done) and agents (who agree to do that work). This theory not only explains the basic relationships but the typical problems (agents who tend to have more information than their principals and principals who therefore have a hard time supervising their agents, known as the "information asymmetry" problem).[72] Second, transaction-cost analysis argues that such information and control problems impose important costs on managers, who naturally seek to minimize their costs while maximizing their gain.[73] Such information problems, if not carefully managed, can cripple managers. While these theories are abstract, they have powerfully and quite explicitly driven reform movements abroad.[74] They have also subtly but clearly flavored both Osborne and Gaebler's *Reinventing Government* and the NPR.

- *Goals.* If basic relationships are contract-like, then the contracts need to be explicit. And if supervision is problematic, supervisors ought to focus instead on the results that their subordinates produce. Performance agreements, based on clear definition of goals, can set the standards by which managers will be judged. In fact, several cabinet secretaries have signed performance agreements with President Clinton. While on one level they are a rhetorical exercise, on a deeper level they represent not only a clear statement of the secretary's goals but also "a leadership commitment to achieving results," as one NPR official explained.[75]

- *Competition.* Even with clear goals, however, managers left to their own devices will tend to under-perform, by substituting leisure or personal goals for the organization's goals (what theorists call the "moral hazard" problem). The information asymmetry problem prevents supervisors from knowing what their subordinates are really doing. Competition (among both employees and organizations, for both pay and other resources) can create strong incentives that can substitute for authority-based supervision.

- *Customers.* No one knows better than customers whether an organization's goals are being met. Driving organizations to serve the customers, from the bottom up, can help solve the supervision problems that plague organizations from the top down.

For government to follow such a prescription, it would have to give more power to front-line workers, focus more clearly on the needs of its customers (leaving aside for a moment the tough problem of defining just who the "customers" are), use the customers to define goals, induce competition to serve these customers, measure results carefully, and stimulate entrepreneurial behavior on the part of government workers everywhere. In fact, that is precisely what the NPR recommended in chapters 2 and 3 of *From Red Tape to Results*.[76] While the theoretical foundation of the NPR is never made explicit, its provenance in the "new economics" approach is clear.

Assessing the Critics

Such arguments, of course, drew much criticism, especially from public administration scholars who rejected the idea that the public and private sectors have anything important in common. In particular, the NPR's critics argued that:

- *Real entrepreneurialism cannot be created in government.* The critics object both to the notion of citizens-as-customers and to the case for entrepreneurialism. H. George Frederickson contends that "governments are not markets" and that "citizens are not the customers. They are the owners."[77] The critics add that, even if entrepreneurialism were a good idea, the concept could never be applied to government. There frequently is little private competition in most public functions.[78] Government exists to take on those jobs that citizens view as important and that the private market cannot or will not assume. Because the public and private sectors are so fundamentally different, entrepreneurial, competitive, private-sector models create more confusion than clarity in public management, the critics conclude.

- *Market incentives cannot substitute for the law.* More fundamentally, they argue that democratic government requires that law, not competition, drive public bureaucracy.[79] The reinventing government argument undermines the constitutional system of top-down democratic accountability. It gives front-line managers too much power to decide for themselves what the law is and how it ought to be executed. That, the critics argue, is a dangerous departure from traditional democratic government, in which power flows from the people to elected officials and from elected officials downward to administrators, under close supervision by superiors. Congress ultimately is the source of administrators' power, yet in the NPR, "Congress is viewed largely as a nuisance," Moe wrote.[80] No matter how inconvenient it might be, the critics strenuously objected to any attempt to substitute market-like behavior for the rule of law.

- *The reinventers undercut critical public management capacity.* In their effort to empower front-line bureaucrats and to meet the administration's downsizing goals, the NPR advocated reducing the number of middle-level managers throughout government to allow managers to manage.[81] OMB followed with a major reorganization that eliminates management analysis as a separate function within the agency (which I will examine later). Such reductions, Frederickson worried, could diminish the government's capacity to function.[82] Moe added that the NPR was a major attack on the "President as Chief Manager."[83] The reduction of central management reinforced the horror of the critics that government would prove unable to manage itself effectively and to hold bureaucrats democratically accountable for their behavior.

- *The real problems are primarily political, not administrative.* Nothing separated the reinventers from their critics more than their analysis of where the core problems lay. For the reinventers, the vision of good people trapped in a bad system — a bad *administrative* system, that is — drove their recommendations. Their critics, on the other hand, defended the administrative system and argued that the problem lay in failures of political judgment and will by elected officials. "The problems are power and politics, not bureaucracy," Frederickson contends.[84] Moe countered that bureaucrats have done their best within a balance-of-power battle between the president and Congress that inevitably undercut their effectiveness.[85] Laurence Lynn adds that the reinventers have also engaged in the folly that technocratic strategies "can somehow short-circuit the political process and be made precise and unambiguous." Efforts to replace politics with management reform, the critics conclude, risk paralyzing the government by weakening political support for administrative leadership.[86]

The academic critics built on long-established traditions in American public administration. Most were Madisonians at heart, so their strongest salvo came against the most Hamiltonian elements of the NPR. Furthermore, they believed that public and private administration were so different that any effort to carry reform ideas (such as customer service and competition) to government from the private sector was both wrong and dangerous. They also believed fundamentally in investment in public management, and in fighting any effort to merge administrative activities into more political decisions (such as the OMB reorganization). Most of all, they build implicitly on long-established traditions of democratic accountability and authority-based/hierarchically organized bureaucracies.

One thread of the critics' attack was telling. The NPR largely ignored fundamental differences between public and private management as well as centuries-old thinking about how to hold bureaucratic power democratically accountable. In particular, the NPR dealt poorly with both the political and the constitutional roles of Congress in American bureaucracy. Finally, the critics struck a telling blow in pointing to the fundamental *political* causes at the root of many *administrative* problems.

However, the academic critics missed two important points. First, existing administrative theory has not served the performance of American government well. The roots of the government's performance problems extend past the political problems into fundamental dysfunctions of the executive branch. Administrative theory does not have a very good diagnosis or prescription to attack these problems. Just how should we understand the connection between political institutions and administrative practice? And how can they mutually support each other to improve government performance?

Second, many of the points that the theorists argued represent problems in theory more than practice. In fact, administrative practices were already far in advance of much theory in the field. Treating citizens as customers *and* as owners, for example, need not be inconsistent (as I will later explain). Entrepreneurial incentives can produce better results within the framework of public law. In Phoenix, for example, Public Works Department workers competed with private contractors for the garbage collection business. In the end, city workers won a sizable share of the work and, under the pressure of competition, greatly increased their productivity.[87]

Much of the criticism grew out of traditional approaches to accountability: legislative supremacy over executive discretion, and administrative action through hierarchical bureaucracy. The problem is that neither approach describes well administrative behavior today. While Congress retains the ultimate power to write the laws that govern bureaucratic behavior, the sources of political influence (over both

Congress and the bureaucracy) are vastly more complex. Moreover, especially at the federal level, little administrative action takes place through traditional hierarchies. Most program implementation depends instead on complex partnerships among federal, state, and local governments, together with private and nonprofit organizations. The critics build at least in part on assumptions about the workings of government that no longer hold. Furthermore, and this is the reinventers' strongest point, they would have little need for a fundamental reinvention if the old theories continued to work well.

There is, in short, a large gap between the theories and the tough realities that government managers must daily face. The managers have not much concerned themselves with the intellectual battles and have struggled to cope pragmatically with the problems they face. But the evidence from the front lines is that such practice is far in front of theory. The theorists, on both sides, badly need to catch up.

Summary

Often overlooked in the hot day-to-day struggles over government reform are the underlying intellectual disputes. It is easy to dismiss the theoretical issues as the province of arcane academics. In reality, ideas matter — matter, in fact, fundamentally.[88] They both drive and steer action. They communicate expectations to bureaucrats together with a sense of the possible. They define the values by which bureaucratic action will be judged. They undergird the symbols by which citizens come to know their government.

Three important theoretical problems plague the NPR. First, compared with the major reforms abroad, the NPR has both a weaker central compass and greater internal intellectual inconsistency in its movement. For better or worse, a reasonably well-articulated philosophy of managerialism and consumerism, for example, has driven reforms in Great Britain, Australia, and New Zealand.[89] This is not a criticism of the NPR. Indeed, its spirit of reform happily collected disparate ideas wherever the reformers found ideas they judged useful. But the NPR has been a set of often very different, sometimes conflicting, ideas flying in only loose formation.

Second, the actions of the NPR have moved far in advance of theory. This is a criticism of the academic community, not of the NPR. Much of administrative theory is locked in a world of hierarchical organization and authority-based control; most of administrative practice, by contrast, builds on cooperative interorganizational networks and negotiation, layered over a legal fabric of hierarchy and authority. Public management theory does not very adequately describe or prescribe the world of the government manager as the nation enters the twenty-first century. Government reform abroad has been widespread, particularly in Australia, New Zealand, Sweden, and the United Kingdom. In the United States, some state and local governments have attempted government reform, while many corporations have launched sweeping efforts. The lessons of these efforts, however, have been fuzzy. On many fronts, the NPR has had to blaze its own trail. This has inevitably led to some wasted effort and unrewarding explorations. Nevertheless, the broad public and specific political support that the NPR has attracted suggests at least that the NPR is focusing on the right questions. The academic community needs to work hard to get back in front of the innovation curve. In particular, we badly need fresh theory on how to achieve democratic accountability in the complex administrative and political world that government managers face. Even more important, we need a new approach to *governance,* to better direct and control the making and administration of public policy.

Third, the combination of these factors has left the reinventers with large mandates supported by mushy thinking. Most noteworthy among these questions are just what "customer service" means, how to define and measure the government's performance, and how to redefine the public interest to fit the new realities of public management. (I will turn to these issues in the next section.) When inevitable questions about these issues emerge, reinventers around government consequently have little clear guidance to fall back on. That, in turn, has fueled the sense of ad hocracy that has often pervaded the NPR, a sense which has only been increased by the frenzy of activity accompanying the reform.

It would be both naive and silly to expect the reinventers, or any other governmental reformers, to work from a textbook. That is not the issue. However, under the banner of *Reinventing Government*, the reinventers have urged government to "steer, not row." With that mandate, the key questions are these: If government *is* to steer, whose hand is on the tiller, and by what compass will the person at the helm steer the ship of state? Who will be doing the rowing, and how?

The question is all the more important because of the NPR's arguments about increasing and decentralizing bureaucratic power. The less central supervision elected officials give operating-level bureaucrats, the more important are the ideas by which they guide their actions. Put differently, *if empowerment drives the NPR, and empowerment means delegating far greater discretion to bureaucrats, what glue will unify governmental policy and prevent it from spinning off centrifugally into thousands of directions?* This is the core problem of accountability in the NPR.

4. Glue: How to Hold the Movement Together?

Two central problems lie at the core of the NPR. First, the NPR is moving far in advance of the ideas driving it. The central themes (cutting red tape, putting customers first, empowering employees, and cutting back to basics) are more a call to arms than a battle plan. Second, especially because the NPR builds on putting far more power in the hands of bureaucrats, the weakness of the battle plan carries grave risks. If empowerment drives the NPR, and empowerment means delegating far greater discretion to bureaucrats, what will direct the exercise of that discretion? What will ensure that bureaucrats use their discretion to promote the public interest instead of simply their own, perhaps idiosyncratic views of what ought to be done? Indeed, an important implication of the economic theory of bureaucracy, on which much of the reinvention movement is based, is that unsupervised bureaucrats will simply pursue their self interest, which in turn will create an ever-growing and ever less efficient government.[90] What glue will unify governmental policy and prevent it from spinning off centrifugally into thousands of directions?

The ultimate success of the NPR depends on solving three important problems: defining a new approach to the public interest, to replace the old version which no longer fits administrative practice or America's political life; sharpening the notion of customer service, to serve as a proximate compass for bureaucratic action; and developing a mature approach to performance measurement, to provide long-term guidance to American public management.

The New Puzzle of the Public Interest

The experiments with government reform in the United States over the last decade teach three important lessons. First, there is no government service that could not be delivered by nongovernmental organizations. From libraries to police, prisons to social services, fire protection to sophisticated planning, private and nonprofit agents have eagerly stepped in as governments have tried to shrink. Although the results of the American version of privatization have varied widely, the overriding lesson is that there is no function left that only the public sector can deliver.[91] However we choose to define what government alone ought to do, we cannot do it by function.[92] The lesson: Because the private sector *can* do anything, we are less sure about what government *ought* to do.

Second, the thrust of government reform has been to impose market-style incentives on public managers. It is the "entrepreneurial spirit" that drives *Reinventing Government,* and for the NPR the keystone of creating a government that works better and costs less is "using market incentives to solve problems."[93] Reformers have argued that competition, rewards, and sanctions will prove far superior to authority-based, monopolistic governmental agencies. In brief, they suggest that many private-sector based mechanisms could usefully replace public-sector oriented mechanisms. The lesson: The debate over incentives has made us less sure about *how* government employees ought to do their jobs.

Finally, the increasing contracting out of government services over the last two decades has increased the mutual dependence of both parties: government on private and nonprofit organizations to deliver services; private and nonprofit organizations on government revenues to sustain their business. In addition, the rules and procedures accompanying the sharing of government's power has created a complex fabric of organizational linkages. The lesson: The harder reformers have tried to separate the public and private sectors, the more blurred the boundaries between them have become.

What these three lessons have created is a fundamental challenge to defining and achieving the public interest. A generation ago, the precepts of traditional public administration made clear what public managers ought to do and how. It was the job of public managers to administer the law by the best of their technical ability. Indeed, in 1950, Leonard D. White could write in the leading textbook of the day:

> The need, incessant and urgent, is for the administrative mind that can hold fast to the public interest and bind conflicting special interests to it by skillful contrivance, based on knowledge but exceeding mere *expertise*. In the highest reaches, the administrative art touches the political, but it grows out of different soil.[94]

In the years that followed, however, the notion that the public interest ought to guide administrative action slowly evaporated as the difficulty of defining it grew. Students of the process worried about the growing complexity of political influences on managers, which created multiple back channels of influence on administrative behavior, and the increasing interconnections among government programs, which made it hard to determine who was responsible for anything.[95] They worried about growing professionalization of the public service, which risked making managers more accountable to narrow professional norms than to the broader goals of the law.[96]

The "public interest" consequently disappeared from most debate about public management: in part because it became so hard to define; in part because some critics wondered if the new entrepreneurial spirit might not be superior to the old notions that drove it. Resurrecting the concept along with the old definitions clearly will not help debate over the NPR. The classical approach does not fit an administrative world of high technology and instantaneous communication, interdependent organizations (public as well as private and nonprofit), and institutionalized political tension between the executive and the legislature.[97]

On the other hand, allowing a careful consideration of the public interest to slip from public discourse risks substituting one set of problems — steering "empowered" bureaucrats — for another — bureaucrats with little incentive for high performance. As Don Hunn, head of New Zealand's Public Service Commission, explains, "We spent so much time trying to 'let the managers manage' that we forgot that government owned these institutions and that there is a set of common, core values." New Zealand, leading the movement for public sector management reform, therefore found itself seeking a new definition of the "collective interest" as a counterpoint to administrative autonomy.[98] Indeed, the New Zealand experience helps chart the mines lying ahead in the NPR's eager push for reinventing government. Sweeping away the old notions of accountability will not work unless something new and equally powerful rises up to replace it.

The success of the NPR depends on establishing and promoting a new definition of the public interest:

- based on a full understanding of how enhanced employee discretion helps government tackle its new challenges better than the old procedure and rule-based approaches;

- based on a sophisticated approach to interorganizational networks of public, private, and nonprofit organizations, instead of the old approach founded on an assumption that a single agency was in charge of each program;

- based on outputs instead of inputs, on results instead of activity;

- based on a fully developed comprehension of what customer service and performance measurement really mean; and

- in particular, based on a fresh but sound approach to ensuring accountability of government workers for the jobs they do: promoting high performance and low cost while remaining responsible to elected officials.

Customer Service

If empowering employees is the "how" of the NPR, customer service is the "why." The reinventers worked from a set of beliefs that drove them away from traditional top-down management: that traditional approaches made bureaucrats unresponsive, self-absorbed, and inefficient. British Prime Minister John Major's 1991 "Citizens Charter" white paper, as well as other movements abroad, heavily flavored the NPR. The reinventers also borrowed from the American private sector reform movement. As Michael Hammer and James Champy put it in their best-seller, *Reengineering the Corporation*:

> The reality that organizations have to confront . . . is that the old ways of doing business — the division of labor around which companies have been organized since Adam Smith first articulated the principle — simply don't work anymore. Suddenly, the world is a different place.[99]

Hammer and Champy argue that dealing with this new world begins with customers, who increasingly know what they want, have choices about how to get it, and do not hesitate to reward companies that deliver with their business. Successful companies are those that build from the top down to serve customers from the bottom up.[100]

The idea of customer service enraged traditionalists, as we saw in the last section. In part, the customer-based approach smacked of importing business management into government, and public management specialists have long held up Wallace Sayre's axiom that business and government are alike in all unimportant respects.[101] In part, they argued that accountability in a democratic republic works from the voters through elected officials to bureaucrats, not directly between citizens-as-customers and government managers. They also quarreled with the drumbeat of customer service rhetoric.

In fact, there are three important conclusions about the customer service idea. First, the critics are right. Government is indeed different from the private sector, and any public sector reform has to begin from that point. Second, there is nevertheless genuine value in the customer service approach. Bureaucrats at every level, throughout every bureaucracy (public or private) have great discretion in how they do their jobs. How, on the margin, should they use that discretion? The customer service notion has great power in answering that question: use the discretion to satisfy citizens rather than serve the purposes of government agencies and employees. Third, the notion nevertheless has proven a weak compass for the NPR. The concept is poorly developed, and over-enthusiastic rhetoric has often substituted for clear thinking. If there is something to customer service, that something needs far more careful development.

The NPR's enthusiasm for customer service builds on the self-evident observation that citizens are truly unhappy with the performance of their government, and that citizens view government as too often pursuing its own internal goals instead of solving the problems of citizens. "Quite simply," the NPR report concludes, "the quality of government service is below what its customers deserve." To solve that problem, the NPR pledged to provide "customer services *equal to the best in business.*"[102] The Social Security Administration, for example, promised that callers to its toll-free service would reach a person on the first call. The Postal Service pledged to deliver first-class mail anywhere in the United States within three days and counter service within five minutes.[103] On September 11, 1993, President Clinton backed that pledge by issuing Executive Order 12862, which mandated agencies to define customer service standards. All executive departments and agencies providing "significant services directly to the public" were required to:

> (a) identify the customers who are, or should be served by the agency;
> (b) survey customers to determine the kind and quality of services they want and their level of satisfaction with existing service;
> (c) post service standards and measure results against them;
> (d) benchmark customer service performance against the best in business;
> (e) survey front-line employees on the barriers to, and ideas for, matching the best in business;
> (f) provide customers with choices in both the sources of service and the means of delivery;
> (g) make information, services, and complaint systems easily accessible; and
> (h) provide means to address customer complaints.

It would be hard for even the most cynical critic to object to serving citizens in this way. As employed by the NPR, "customer service" essentially requires that government be responsive to citizens' needs and wants. The presumption is that too often government becomes inward-directed, toward the myriad rules, procedures, and forms that preoccupy public managers. Forcing these managers to focus outward on citizens, for whom public programs were originally created, is intended as an antidote. Such an approach is consistent with traditional theories of accountability.

The executive order does not call for the exercise of discretion beyond the boundaries of existing law. Rather, it calls for government employees to use the inevitable discretion embodied in congressional delegation of authority to ensure that government services are responsive to citizens. As *Improving Customer Service*, a report accompanying the NPR, concluded, customer service "is probably the simplest way to tell the federal work force what kind of service to deliver."[104]

Indeed, some of the most spectacular early successes of the NPR came from reinvention labs that dramatically improved customer service. In the Department of Veterans Affairs claims processing center in New York, for example, the manager set out to improve service to veterans. Workers previously had focused narrowly on specialized parts of the claim process. Veterans were no more than numbers, and the lack of coordination among the pieces of the process produced long delays in processing checks. The manager reorganized part of his staff into a team comprised of each of the specialties required to process a claim. Team members focused on each individual veteran and worked together to solve the veterans' problems. Processing time dropped from years to weeks or months. The job satisfaction of the workers improved and the veterans were much happier with the friendly and prompt action on their claims. Focusing on the customer — how can the process be organized around the needs of the veteran? — instead of process — how can we most easily process this paper? — dramatically improved the office's performance.[105]

The NPR, in fact, has helped launch several such customer service initiatives, including one-stop career centers in the Department of Labor's Employment and Training Administration and improvements to the Treasury Bureau of Engraving and Printing's public tours. These experiments demonstrate that customer service need not be incompatible with bureaucratic accountability — responsibility of bureaucrats to elected officials for the management of their programs. In fact, customer service can improve accountability while it increases satisfaction. Frederickson has noted that citizens are owners, not customers.[106] However, even owners appreciate being treated responsively as customers. A stockholder (that is, owner) of an automobile company, for example, certainly expects responsiveness when entering a car dealership. Indeed, the stockholder's concern for the bottom line can even increase concern about the quality of customer service.

The real problem with the NPR's customer service initiative is not that it is incompatible with democratic accountability. Rather, the notion of customer service in government itself is so new the concept is underdeveloped. Using the idea to drive bureaucratic performance therefore requires substantial intellectual innovation which, to date, has not accompanied the NPR. Moreover, as currently employed, it is a crude fit at best for what government does and how it does it, for three reasons.

1. Multiple goals. Responsiveness to citizens is not the only, or even the principal, goal of public programs.[107] As service recipients, citizens naturally expect responsiveness: prompt, friendly, and generous service. The road that, in a big snowstorm, needs to be plowed first is always in front of one's own home. As taxpayers, however, they demand economy and efficiency from government. "Pork-barrel programs" are programs given to someone else. Responsiveness to citizens as service recipients inevitably and eternally conflicts with the demands of citizens-as-taxpayers. Government managers therefore tend to face greater demands than they can ever possibly meet and clashing views about how to meet them. Should the Interior Department reintroduce gray wolves into Yellowstone National Park, as environmentalists have advocated, or should it try to clean out the wolves, to satisfy ranchers?[108] Should the Federal Aviation Administration supervise new but small airlines relatively more, on the grounds that with less experience they might have greater problems? Or should they focus relatively more attention on the older but larger carriers that transport far more travelers? The question is even worse in welfare programs. Should the Department of Health and Human Services seek to make it as easy and painless as possible for Medicaid recipients to qualify for health care? Or should the department attempt to manage the program as strictly as possible to reduce costs?

Such conflicts create a dilemma for bureaucrats attempting to follow the customer service mantra. If they concentrate solely on responsiveness to citizens as service recipients, and therefore seek to maximize the services they deliver, they risk conflict with citizens as taxpayers. If they try to satisfy citizens as taxpayers, and therefore seek to deliver a minimal level of services, they risk disappointing citizens as service recipients. Asking government bureaucrats, within the realm of their discretion, to pursue both efficiency and responsiveness creates an impossible problem. And leaving bureaucrats with impossible problems in the end only further increases their discretion and the difficulty of holding them accountable to either the law or customer service standards.

The more hopeful side of customer service is that bureaucrats inevitably have substantial discretion. The broad promises and vague guidance of most acts of Congress leave them considerable maneuvering room in doing their jobs. The customer service movement argued that bureaucrats, in exercising that discretion, ought to put citizens' needs foremost. Their job is, at its core, to administer the law and maximize the use of available resources. But in deciding just *how* to do that, the movement contends, bureaucrats should focus on their customers. The question is whether more federal employees can be persuaded to find a balance among the competing demands on their time and energy that makes it easier for citizens to deal with their government.

2. Connecting with the customer. Second, many federal programs — and most federal bureaucrats — do not provide "significant services directly to the public," in the words of the executive order. There are, to be sure, federal programs and bureaucrats that do have substantial contact with citizens: air traffic control, patrol of waterways, operation of dams, operation of social security, customs collection, the national parks. But the nature of many federal functions and the complexity of program implementation both create large challenges for customer service.

Some government functions, like regulation, tax collection, and criminal justice, present tough customer service problems. Government officials must find the difficult balance between making their programs user-friendly and preventing abuse. Nevertheless, the IRS has devoted itself to making its tax forms more user-friendly and to improving the quality of telephone tax advice. The Customs Service in Miami has received one of Vice President Gore's "Hammer Awards" for improving service for the airlines and their passengers. There has even been tentative discussion about applying the customer service approach to prisons to reduce violence and costs. The ingenuity of both the reformers and government managers has been remarkable, but the underlying fact is that the nature of many government functions makes pursuing customer service far more difficult than the rhetoric suggests.

Working through the long and complex implementation chain of most federal programs presents additional challenges. Most federal government employees never encounter a citizen while performing their official duties. Their job, rather, is to help others do their job so that citizens, eventually, are served. It is not unusual, for example, for a federal manager to distribute a grant to a state agency, which adds state money and state requirements and then passes it on to a local agency, which then contracts out to a nonprofit organization to actually deliver the service to a citizen — who then must negotiate a system providing related services through similar complex relationships. It is, quite often, a government by proxy.[109] It is the job of the federal employee to work with the next person in the chain (whether another federal employee, a state government worker, perhaps a private contractor). Under such circumstances, it is easy for the citizen-as-customer's concerns to get lost.[110] It is also easy for everyone along the chain to claim innocence for how the citizen is handled. If everyone is in charge, no one has responsibility for results. Making customer service work means focusing everyone along the chain on how well the system works (or does not) for the ultimate recipient of services. It also means orienting their actions to improve the odds that citizens' needs, not the internal needs of workers in the chain, are served.

In July 1994, Oregon officials proposed a novel, head-on attack against these system problems. State officials proposed shifting the intergovernmental programs targeted at Oregon from an agency- and program-based effort to one focused on results. The plan, developed by government officials in Oregon, would begin by having the federal government join with Oregon state and local governments to "identify results to be achieved." From there, the Oregon officials suggested,

> we will be contracted to achieve them. To help us achieve these results, the federal government will merge funding categories and streams, create funding incentives which reward desirable results, and reduce micromanagement and wasteful paperwork. This collaboration will empower our communities to identify local needs to be met by federal and state programs, to make their own decisions about how to address those needs, and to be accountable for results.[111]

The state had already developed a twenty-year strategic plan, with specific benchmarks (quantified policy objectives) defined.[112] Its officials argued that its basic approach (defining goals, building programs around people instead of levels of government, and constructing the system to serve those goals and people) fit into the NPR's philosophy. Furthermore, they contended, their approach would cut through the barriers that hindered "efficiency, integrated, client-centered service."[113] Although the proposal was embryonic, it attracted widespread interest in Washington. The meeting in Washington to discuss it attracted top officials from OMB, the Departments of Health and Human Services, Education, and Labor, and 170 other senior agency staff from around the capital. To many observers and participants, it suggested an alternative solution to the intergovernmental dilemma: to focus on outcomes instead of inputs and on people instead of programs, and to use that approach to transform the organizational arrangements. Armed with a different way of seeing the problem, they hoped, the reformers argued that they might be able to crack the old quandary.

3. Hypersensitivity to customer wishes. Finally, a large part of government's performance problem is a hypersensitivity, not an insensitivity, to the demands of citizens. Elected officials, indeed, are preoccupied with the demands of their constituents. They have few incentives to worry about broad public management issues like performance, quality, or cost; they have every incentive to deliver the goods, from new dams to protection for social security, to the voters. That problem led George Frederickson to argue, tongue only partially in cheek, that real reform lies in employing "total quality politics," not "total quality management."[114] The danger, and it is the most subtle yet most important element of the customer service initiative, is that customer focus on the part of government managers could reinforce the constituent-based pressure of elected officials and produce a government hyper-tuned to micro-level needs yet without capacity or incentive to deliver broad or sustained performance.[115]

This is not a case against customer service but a brief for thinking it through thoroughly and implementing it carefully. That, however, has not yet happened in the NPR. The customer service initiative has proven little more than an executive order demanding action and a rhetorical flag under which virtually any enterprise can operate. The British, in fact, have considerably more experience with the customer service notion. Their experiences teach several important lessons.[116]

- Defining customers is much harder than it looks. Different people tend to want very different things, and these preferences are not easily aggregated.

- A focus on customers — users of services — tends to avoid the question of who ought to pay for services. It can even accentuate the taxpayer versus service recipient dilemma.

- A service-based approach works poorly for public goods, like defense and pollution control, for which it is impossible to define individual beneficiaries.[117] A large share of the federal government's activities, of course, center on such public goods.

- The customer service approach encourages individuals to develop, express, and advocate preferences just as government's ability to satisfy them shrinks under the weight of fiscal stress.

- Excessive zeal in measuring citizen preferences can produce an information overload.

- Customer service can easily be put to partisan use. Critics of the party in power have used information about citizen complaints to attack the party. This, naturally, leads the ruling party to collect information most likely to put programs in a favorable light. Many elected officials complain about spending any money for citizen surveys.

Customer service is an undeniably attractive notion. Making government fit citizens' needs better is an inescapable imperative. But the notion raises as many problems as it solves. Customer service does, however, have two overriding values. It gears "the organization to serve its public rather than the other way around," as one participant in the British effort explained.[118]

It also provides a fresh approach to the eternal search for the Holy Grail of program coordination. No one can spend much time with federal managers without sensing their frustration. The budget cuts of the 1980s have trimmed both people and resources from their agencies. To compensate, most managers have struggled to improve their operations to the point where many believe that there are few additional savings to be wrung out. (Notable exceptions to this point are "high-risk" areas that pose substantial managerial and budgetary problems. I will return to them later.) They have increasingly come to believe that the next generation of front-line reforms will come from improving the wiring *between* agencies and programs, not within them. That, in fact, is the focus of several reinvention labs, the Department of Agriculture's rural development initiative,[119] and the state of Oregon's initiative to improve intergovernmental partnerships.

The customer service initiative therefore has enormous potential. It is most useful as a proximate goal in directing the exercise of bureaucratic discretion. It can never fully steer government action, however, in part because of the inherent contradictions rooted deeply in the concept and in part because at best it is only a weak guide. A far more important and useful guide for government action is performance management. Developing a robust performance system, however, will take years, as I show in the next section. In the meantime, customer service can be a road in the same direction. Even achieving that more limited potential, however, will require a far more sophisticated exploration of what customer service means, how to do it, and how to fit it within the demands and constraints of democratic government. (The Australians, for example, are defining the competencies required for high-quality customer service. See appendix I.) It also requires a frank admission of the value conflicts and dilemmas that the customer service initiative will surface. The NPR has done neither, and without taking both steps the drive toward customer service will suffer.

Performance Management

In the long run, building a government that works better and costs less depends on strengthening OMB's ability to guide it. If government is to steer effectively, OMB will have to stand at the helm. But for OMB to steer, it will have to have a compass more precise and more far reaching than annual review of the budgetary process. It needs a mature performance management system to assess what government actually accomplishes with taxpayers' money.

The most promising source of glue to hold the movement together and promote the right incentives lies in the Office of Management and Budget: the reorganization of the agency launched in March 1994 under the banner of "OMB 2000"; and the Government Performance and Results Act (GPRA), passed in 1993, which seeks to link budget inputs with performance outcomes. The OMB 2000 reorganization was, quite simply, the most fundamental change in the agency since its creation. OMB Director Leon Panetta and Deputy Director Alice Rivlin forcefully argued the need to escape from routine budget reviews and to "better integrate our budget analysis, management review and policy development roles."[120] The reorganization eliminated virtually all of the existing "management side" of OMB and integrated management functions with the budget review in new "resource management offices."[121] These new offices would be responsible for formulating and reviewing the budget, assessing program effectiveness and efficiency, conducting mid- and long-range policy and program analysis, implementing government-wide management policy in areas like procurement and financial management, and conducting program evaluation. OMB created five resource management offices: National Security and International Affairs; Natural Resources, Energy and Science; Health and Personnel; Human Resources; and General Government.[122]

OMB 2000 sought to help the budget agency move from the deadlines and short time horizons of the annual budget process to a longer-term results-oriented perspective. OMB officials said they wanted "to be more strategic in the way we prepare the budget."[123] Some analysts have harshly criticized the reorganization because it eliminated the management arm.[124] However, the management division within OMB had long been a weak player, especially in overseeing general management issues. OMB officials had only two real options: pursuing the reorganization to provide integrated analysis, but risk having short-term budget issues drive out long-term management concerns; or create a separate office of federal management to assess administrative issues, but risk having the office become a eunuch in a setting where budgetary decisions inevitably drive policy.[125] Faced with these choices, Panetta and Rivlin followed the first option.

The reorganization promised several important innovations. First, it provided a linkage between budgetary and management issues which previously had been fragmentary at best. Second, it committed OMB to adopt a broader and longer perspective on budget and management issues. Third, it provided the potential for integrating performance questions into the annual budgetary process (although the ambitious plan had no clear implementation plan). Finally, it sought to change the language of communication between OMB and the agencies. By raising its sights from narrow budgetary issues to larger performance issues, OMB sought to change the incentives for the way departmental budget officers communicated their requests.

The reorganization was ambitious; transforming the deep-seated budget-review culture was a huge job. OMB also faced a big problem of training its budget examiners in how to take the broader view and of integrating its management experts into the resource management offices without undercutting their morale. OMB was never successful in combining management and budget analysis in the same agency. Nor was it ever truly successful in combining long-term strategic planning with short-term attention to details. OMB 2000 attempts both tough jobs, but this time makes the transformation within people, especially budget examiners, instead of their organizational structure. One risk is that the short-term focus of the annual budget process will drive out careful attention to the more long-term management issues. Another risk is that OMB's historical focus on money and inputs will drive out attention to administration and outputs.

In the best of cases, OMB will acquire the capacity to link outputs and inputs, budget and management. In the worse of cases, central attention to federal management will disappear from the top circle in government. And that is something that cannot be allowed to happen. If the challenges are great, however, the direction is sound. The annual budget process remains the single most important way of focusing the attention of federal managers at every level. Transforming that process offers the most important way of transforming the behavior of those managers.

OMB's reorganization was designed to support GPRA. GPRA is part of a far wider movement, in both the United States and abroad, to focus managers' attention on accountability for results. It aimed at improving the effectiveness of federal programs and citizen satisfaction by improving "the confidence of the American people in the capability of the Federal Government, by systematically holding Federal agencies accountable for achieving program results."[126] In the long run, moreover, GPRA may well prove to be the keystone of the federal government's reinvention movement. It defines performance as the critical touchstone of the government's programs; it defines the linkages among the government's activities; and it provides important incentives for government managers to focus on results. Under the act, each federal agency, by the end of the ten-year phase-in period, will prepare:

- a five-year strategic plan, that is updated every three years;

- a comprehensive mission statement that links the agency's current operations with its long-term goals;

- an identification of the goals and objectives, along with the resources, systems, and processes required to achieve the goals;

- a description of the most important external factors that could affect the agency's success in achieving the goals; and

- annual program evaluations to help agency officials assess their success, explain why goals might not have been met, and revise the goals if necessary.

OMB and the president would then use the process to set future budgets and to revise programs, if necessary. The law called for at least ten pilot projects. By the summer of 1994, federal agencies had put forward seventy-one pilots in twenty-one departments and agencies.[127]

OMB did not expect the transition to performance-based management to come easily. In their briefing documents, OMB officials asserted that change will require a long-term process, even though they quickly encouraged performance measures as part of agency budget submissions.[128] This process, in turn, required fundamental changes in the culture of government management and the assumption of more responsibility by managers throughout the government. OMB officials, in fact, repeatedly stressed that agency officials would be the leaders in GPRA. They did not intend for this to be a top-down management reform.

Most important, GPRA depends on technology that does not now exist. There is no budgetary system, no performance measurement system, and no career track within government for the people to do the work. There are few incentives for such a long-range perspective, and only a passing audience among elected officials, citizens, and the media for the results.[129] That is not a prescription for failure, but it is a measure of the work to be done if the promise of GPRA is to be met.

The federal government's ragged experience with management and reform, from planning-programming-budgeting and management by objectives through zero-based budgeting and total quality management, suggests caution in pressing ahead without building the technology for GPRA. But several things are clearly different this time. First, this is the first of the reforms launched by law instead of executive order or administrative action. GPRA's base in law ensures both congressional and executive branch involvement and makes it harder for its sponsors to retreat.

Second, unlike previous reforms that began with an across-the-board effort, GPRA builds slowly from pilot programs to governmentwide implementation. This provides an opportunity for learning along the way.

Third, the early evidence suggests that this reform enjoys far broader and more enthusiastic support throughout the bureaucracy than earlier efforts. The surprising eagerness of federal agencies to volunteer for the pilot phase of the act underlined the eagerness of federal managers and top political appointees to grab the leverage that GPRA offered.

Finally, GPRA speaks with unusual clarity to problems that citizens want to have solved. It would be hard to find anyone who finds government performance satisfactory, or that linking budgets with results is not a good idea. The 1992 Perot presidential campaign underlined that point.

Like the OMB 2000 reorganization, GPRA offered considerable promise for linking the big politics of reducing the size of government and the little politics of improving its performance. OMB 2000 potentially provides the incentive for agencies to pay more attention to performance; GPRA provides the language to discuss it. Past experience with aggressive budget and management reforms argues for caution in predicting results. If the NPR is to have lasting meaning, however, linking the two revolutions is critical. If joined, they offer substantial potential.

The problem is that it is far easier to talk about performance management than to do it. Goals are notoriously difficult to define. Greater specificity regularly attracts greater political conflict. Moreover, even if goals can somehow be made clear, measuring progress is even harder. Public programs are public often because the private sector cannot or will not produce them. The very nature of public programs typically makes outcomes even harder to judge. Managers often have little choice but to substitute input or activity measures (money spent or people served) for outcome measures (what the money accomplishes).

If the technical problems of measuring progress can be surmounted, building the capacity throughout the government to do the job is difficult indeed, especially with the NPR's pledge to shrink the federal bureaucracy by 272,900 positions within five years. OMB has pledged to attack the job by merging its budget and management staffs into "resource management offices," but the critical problem there is the old one: ensuring that short-term budget demands do not drive out assessment of long-term management problems. And if measures emerge, comparing data across widely different programs is a daunting job. How can decisionmakers compare the results of health programs against highway construction, social security against defense?

Finally, even if results can be measured and compared with goals, it is hard to gain an audience for the findings. Elected officials frequently gain far more value by supporting new programs than by overseeing performance.[130] Administrators have few incentives for allowing anyone to measure what they actually do.

Nearly everyone agrees that "the budget process is not likely to be changed substantially until and unless decisionmakers use information on program performance when making allocation decisions," as the Congressional Budget Office argued.[131] Only by changing the incentives for managers, by focusing members of Congress on performance issues when they make budgetary decisions, will performance management become a reality. The difficulty is that elected officials understandably concentrate far more on the front end of the process. Even if measuring performance were easy, changing the political culture to focus on outcomes runs against the driving incentives of the American system. And measuring performance is decidedly not easy. If it were, it would not have taken the federal government decades to commit itself to the effort — and then to give itself another decade to put the idea into place.

Summary

The biggest difficulty in thinking through the problems of performance management is that reformers and managers alike far too often consider it simply as a problem of *measurement*. Committing the government to performance-based management, of course, requires that officials throughout government identify and measure results. The more fundamental question, however, is what we will do with these measures. Too often, reformers pursue measurement for its own sake. If that becomes the case with GPRA, then it will simply become a new procedural shibboleth to replace an old one. It will become a fresh symptom of the program it was designed to solve.

Performance-based management is most fundamentally about *communication*, not measurement. Moreover, this communication occurs within a broader political process, in which the players have a wide array of different incentives. Performance-based management will have meaning only to the degree to which it shapes and improves those incentives. If we think about performance-based management only as a measurement problem — how can we gauge the results that public programs produce? — we will miss the big questions: How does what we know about results shape how we manage public programs? How does our knowledge about results shape decisions about what programs we ought to adopt? And how does the process of measuring results affect the behavior of political institutions?

This leads to several important lessons for GPRA:

- *Performance measurement is different at different levels of the bureaucracy.* While front-line supervisors might be interested in assessing the quality of work done by their subordinates, higher-level officials are likely to want to judge the quality of their programs. Top administration officials and members of Congress will be looking not only at program performance but where they can squeeze out extra performance for the same amount of money, cut spending without losing as much performance, or guess what additional results they will buy with extra money. In short, debate at the political level revolves around broad strategic measures and outcomes. On the front lines, supervisors focus on outputs. Managers in between need to build the linkage between these very different questions.[132] Measures that work at one level will not necessarily work well at another.

- *Aggregating performance measures from lower levels is likely to produce meaningless noise.* A huge temptation in performance measurement is to layer performance measures from lower levels on top of each other and pass the information along to higher-level officials. Such an approach will not only produce information that will not be easily digestible by top officials. It also creates the potential for burying officials in paper and hiding embarrassing details in a mountain of data. Officials at each level will have to define the kind of information they find most useful.

- *Performance measurement will have to speak in a language that those listening can understand.* Too often analysts who conduct sophisticated analysis complain that top managers and elected officials pay no attention to their work. This is much like English-speaking tourists complaining, on visiting the Great Wall of China, that no one understands their requests for directions. If performance measurement is to be a successful language for political communication, it will have to be a language that those listening, especially busy elected officials and top political appointees, will understand and find useful. Indeed, those crafting the measures will have to work carefully to craft the measures to serve their customers. And customer-sensitive lower-level managers will have to anticipate what kind of information their superiors will need, and in what form they can most easily present the data.

- *Performance measurement, moreover, must speak in a language that those listening will want to hear.* There is a special problem in speaking performance information to Congress. Congress naturally tends to think of solving problems by passing laws; indeed, that is its Constitutional charge. That makes Congress peculiarly input-oriented. Its oversight, moreover, tends to be haphazard and episodic. It has few incentives for regular and systematic review.[133] Performance measurement, on the other hand, seeks a careful and systematic survey of results. Performance measurers must find a way to interest members of Congress in GPRA and the results it produces. It will have little staying power otherwise.

Put simply, performance measurement is about political communication. It has value only to the degree to which it improves communication. A careful look at performance measurement, therefore, naturally includes a searching analysis of what we know about measuring results. But it must also include a thoughtful examination of how the process of measuring results will enter the political discourse, and how it will shape the behavior of the players in the political process.

5. Missing Pieces

Despite the encyclopedic coverage of the NPR's report and the sweeping actions that followed, several important issues either are missing or have received scant attention. Without attacking and solving these missing pieces of the picture, the NPR risks undercutting its promise.

Civil Service

Reforming the civil service flows as a theme throughout the NPR report, and changing the rules of the civil service has been a major focus for much of the NPR's work since. However, as discussed in section 2, creating a government that works better and costs less will depend ultimately on the movement's ability to build the capacity to do the job. Government's problem is a people problem as well as a process problem. Real reform hinges on government's ability to find, attract, promote, train, guide, and motivate the workers needed to do its work. Major pieces are missing from the NPR's personnel reform effort, and without them the movement will not have the capacity to accomplish its goals.

Investment

The NPR has great promise for cutting the costs of government. To produce some of these cost savings, however, the federal government will have to make short-term investments if the long-term results are to materialize, as the NPR's report recognized.[134] In its first year, however, the incessant drive for deficit reduction has pushed the investment initiative off the stage. The different pieces of the NPR are, in many ways, an inseparable package. The reengineering of the federal government anticipates that advanced technology will make it possible to reduce the number of workers. The number of workers, though, is being reduced far in advance of even the promise of new investment. The risk is that the NPR will deliver a government that, in the long run, costs more and works worse.

Steering

If the government's job is to steer, as Osborne and Gaebler suggest, whose hand will be on the tiller? Reforms abroad, in state and local governments, and even the reinvention experience at the federal level to date all reinforce the same point: Not only is strong political leadership necessary; there also has to be central administrative capacity to connect the person at the helm with the rowing mechanisms. To prevent the creation of a new government agency, NPR officials deliberately decided not to make the NPR an agency. Instead, the NPR has been staffed by detailees from other agencies rotating in and (often) out. Consequently few hands have been on board since the beginning. Meanwhile, OPM and OMB are undergoing major changes in mission and organization, and the General Services Administration is transforming its procurement functions and processes. All of the federal government's central management agencies are thus simultaneously undergoing major changes. The signals to managers throughout government therefore are unavoidably fuzzy and, sometimes, inconsistent.

The question for the NPR is not the instability. Considerable confusion is inevitable in any reform of this size, and the experience of other nations suggests that it will take at least two or three more years for stable patterns even to begin to emerge. Rather, the question is who will ultimately be responsible for maintaining the reform movement. The NPR has implicitly answered the question. There will be no central steering mechanism. The NPR report talked about the need for central management agencies to divest themselves of many of their powers, to decentralize those powers to the agencies, and thereby to empower workers. While this is a sensible beginning tactic, it is no basis on which to build long-term success. Practical politics suggests that, when problems or embarrassments arise from the behavior of empowered managers, as inevitably they will, predictable demands will surface that they never be allowed to occur again. In the absence of stronger forces to the contrary, someone at some central office will be charged, by the president and/or Congress, with doing just that. Practical management also suggests that it is unlikely that the accumulated decisions of millions of empowered workers will be consistent with each other, the law, or the public interest.

If government is to steer, someone will have to keep the compass. This does not mean the creation or reinforcement of large, overbearing central bureaucracies. It does not mean turning OMB into a lion or GSA into a micro-level investigator. But it does require careful thought about which functions (particularly information collection, long-range assessment, problem solving, coordination, and the articulation of driving themes) inevitably need to be central ones. We can safely predict that these, and perhaps others, *will* occur. The question is where and by whom. The NPR can avoid the question and risk having others answer it in ways that might contradict the movement's principles. Or the NPR can aggressively seek to answer it and fix central responsibility clearly. The issue is not *whether* the answer will emerge; it is *how*, whether implicitly or explicitly, in support of or opposed to the movement that the NPR has labored to launch.

The logic of my argument for the OMB 2000 reorganization plan and GPRA is that the budget office is the natural, perhaps inevitable, place for these questions to be answered. Indeed, the NPR's recommendations, OMB's reorganization, and GPRA's long-term strategic planning and performance measurement requirements all are mutually supporting. The reinvented OMB is the logical place for the central steering role to occur, and it is time now to begin planning the transition from the NPR's short-term, jump-starting role to OMB's long-term nurturing and maintenance role.

Congress

When Clinton administration officials released the NPR report in September 1993, they received at least grudging support from Capitol Hill. Most members of Congress recognized the appeal of a government that works better and costs less. In the details, however, Congress reverted to form.[135] Its members supported the rhetoric in general but micromanaged the details. On one hand, Congress enthusiastically endorsed the downsizing initiative and even upped the ante from a cut of 252,000 government workers to 272,900. Members eagerly calculated how to spend the savings on the crime bill. When it came to individual decisions to produce the savings, however, Congress quickly retreated. They not only voted to exempt favored departments from downsizing. They also torpedoed the Department of Labor's plan to combine 154 federal job training programs, housed in fourteen different federal agencies, into a coordinated effort.[136]

These actions teach an important lesson. Although NPR officials long contended that they could launch most of their reforms without Congress, the reality is that the NPR cannot sustain *any* of its reforms without congressional support, or at least the absence of opposition.[137] NPR officials began their reforms without a strategy for winning that support (or defusing that opposition) beyond the brave hope that the overwhelming logic of the reform would bring members of Congress to their camp. They have been struggling ever since, from the buyout bill through procurement reform, to recover.

Congress, by practice and the Constitution, attacks problems by passing laws. The NPR seeks to solve problems by improving performance. Congress as an institution works on the input side. The NPR focuses on the output side. Congress has little incentive to worry about results and, in fact, has long indulged itself in a separation-of-powers fantasy that absolves it from any complicity in the executive branch's performance problems. Members of Congress, furthermore, have everything to gain from publicly embracing the broad principles of reinvention and then protecting their constituents and favorite programs behind the scenes in committee rooms and little-noticed riders to complex bills. If problems later develop, they will have been the result of a misdirected executive branch.

The NPR, however, has several advantages to tackle these problems. Many of the recommendations in the report, and much of its broad philosophical flavoring of performance and customer service, are of remote interest to most members of Congress. Congressional disinterest gives the reinventers a great deal of initial maneuvering room to prove the success of their effort. Moreover, many of the recommendations depend on how individual bureaucrats deal daily with issues on their desks and the discretion they have to solve problems. That is particularly true of customer service and program coordination issues. They can make substantial progress by changing the way they do business, without changing the business they are in.

The NPR's long-term success nevertheless depends on creating at least some incentives for members of Congress in the reinvention process. The biggest incentive would be clear evidence that government does indeed work better and cost less, although that would scarcely prevent members of Congress from tinkering with details to benefit their constituents. Even that, however, has lost some of its appeal, for local television reporters and newspaper columnists across the country have begun to point out the hypocrisy of embracing broad reforms while undermining them with pork-barrel votes, even if the pork is flowing back home. Many members of Congress are struggling with some way to make government, and therefore their own jobs, more palatable to voters. They are seeking ways to wring extra performance out of government so there will at least be a small amount of money to spend on new programs.

Furthermore, some members of Congress from committees that have long been relatively dormant, like the House Government Operations Committee and the Senate Governmental Affairs Committee, have discovered that the NPR has given them new, high-profile issues like procurement reform and performance measurement. In an era when fiscal constraints prevent most committees from taking major initiatives, these high-profile issues have given some members new standing. Because they cut across so many government programs and agencies — that is, because they cut across the jurisdictions of so many other congressional committees — these issues have also created the potential for new power centers in Congress.

Much of this rationale is tentative or hypothetical. The important point, however, is that the NPR creates subtle opportunities for building congressional support for its initiatives. It would be folly to think that members of Congress will put pork-barrel incentives aside. It would also be folly to ignore the fact that most members of Congress are having far less fun than they used to, and many members are hungrily looking for some way to improve the way government works. The NPR is rich with potential, but congressional support will not naturally flow to it any more than water will naturally flow uphill. Still, with careful strategy and the construction of new mechanisms, water can indeed be made to flow uphill — and the NPR can build congressional support for its initiatives. Given the slow start, however, the task is now all the greater.

High-Risk Programs

The NPR paid scant attention to the government's "high-risk programs," identified by both OMB and the General Accounting Office (GAO), which have the potential for costing the federal government billions of dollars.[138] The Department of Energy (DOE), for example, has more than $19 billion in contracts under management by major firms and academic organizations. The NPR recommended that DOE improve its contract management, but the steps required do not fit neatly into the NPR approach. GAO found that

> Historically, Energy's contractors have operated largely without oversight of financial risk, and this has placed the government's multibillion-dollar annual investment in contractors' services at risk. Energy lacks the necessary staff expertise and information systems to monitor contractors, and its contracts provide few incentives for cost-effective contractor operations.

The core of the problem, GAO found, lay in DOE's own administrative capacity and in the nature of the contracts it negotiated.[139] Neither issue received major attention in the NPR. Most of the NPR's procurement focus lay in untying the red tape binding the procurement process. DOE's fundamental problems stemmed from precisely the opposite problem: the government's over-reliance on private markets.[140] The same is true of many other high-risk programs identified by OMB and GAO, from Medicare to Superfund. The lesson is that by squeezing money out of the federal budget by under-investing in management, poorly managed federal programs have cost taxpayers dearly.[141] Problems have plagued the Environmental Protection Agency Superfund program. DOE has made only halting progress in cleaning up its nuclear weapons facilities despite spending vast sums of money. Management problems in both cases have cost billions of dollars.[142]

In fact, it is a safe bet that savings from solving these and other management problems would swamp the savings promised through the NPR. Money saved by avoiding future management problems, however, will not show up on the budget as savings. It cannot be scored by CBO. Nor can members of Congress take credit for saving it or turn around and spend the savings elsewhere. The money saved is real, but expenses forgone do not travel politically as well as bureaucrats shown the door.

The high-risk problems stem from causes rooted deeply in the government's personnel, financial management, and contract management systems, and they cannot readily be fixed through culture change, empowerment, customer service, or the NPR's other themes. Moreover, the short-term tactical decisions the NPR made to press the movement ahead, particularly downsizing the federal work force, risks making the high-risk problems even worse. By cutting to a target instead of to a plan, the downsizing could easily eliminate both the people and the skills needed to attack the problem. And the long-run costs could dwarf the short-term budget savings. The NPR needs to examine its strategy carefully to ensure it includes a focused attack on the high-risk programs.

Learning

One of the most remarkable features of the NPR is just how much positive activity it generated the first year. And no part of that activity has been more remarkable than the inventiveness thousands of government employees across the country have shown in the reinvention labs. The NPR has worked hard to gather success stories from these labs. A series of new electronic networks has encouraged managers to share results, but the NPR's learning strategy is embryonic. There has been little systematic effort to learn what the labs, or the broader reinvention movement, have to teach.[143]

For example, the Department of Veterans Affairs Contract Service Center reinvention lab in Milwaukee teaches several important lessons. Its staff has been working since 1992 to improve procurement for eight VA hospitals in three states. One of the department's respiratory therapists noted that the VA was paying for full refills of home oxygen tanks even if the tanks were still half full. In a new contract the lab negotiated, the VA specified that it would pay only for the oxygen actually used, and the department saved $100,000 per year. Since its start, Milwaukee officials estimate that through this and similar reforms they have saved $1 million.[144]

The NPR argued that procurement decisions would work best by decentralizing decisions as much as possible, and indeed the Milwaukee lab works in part by decentralizing contract legal review and approval authority from Washington to the field. However, the Milwaukee lab also *centralized* contract authority from the hospitals to a regional facility. That allowed larger buys and, therefore, better economies of scale. It allowed improved record keeping so that the office could better monitor the performance of contractors, and it allowed the office to assemble skilled employees to manage the technical side of the purchases. The lab followed only part of the reinvention prescription, learned some new lessons, and has important lessons to teach. The NPR, however, has devised no way to reach out, collect the information, digest it, and figure out how to sharpen the principles of reinvention.

Summary

Even though the NPR covered an enormous range of the federal government's activities, it nevertheless left several large and important gaps. Some of the gaps involved potential for significant dollar losses that could swamp the cost savings the NPR promised. Some involved the potential for politically undermining the reinvention movement. And some undercut the movement's ability to learn from its own successes. Plugging the gaps is critical to the NPR's long-term success.

Conclusion

In just its first year, the NPR has confounded its critics. It has accomplished far more than cynics suggested might be possible. It has also launched, for the most part, a broad reform movement in the right direction. If the NPR has not always had clear answers, it has been at least asking the right questions. Nevertheless, and this is the NPR's critical problem, the short-term accommodations it inevitably needed to make to get the movement going have weakened the NPR's chances for long-term success. It is now not a self-sustaining revolution, and considerable work needs to be done to move the invasion from a beachhead to a breakout, and then from a breakout to conquest.

Reinventing government centers on the intersection of the "high politics" of presidential-congressional struggles and the "low politics" of routine administration.[145] The connections between policymaking and execution, what we often call "governance" — are indisputably fraying. The question is where the problem lies: with good people trapped in a bad system, as the reinventers claim, or with a good system hamstrung by a failure of political leadership, as the movement's critics assert? The critics contend that, in the mad rush of the Clinton administration's "high politics" ambitions, the reinventers have misunderstood the foundations on which democratic administration rests. They argue that the reinventers have no theory but a set of unspoken assumptions which, if exposed, would reveal the movement as a threat to democratic governance. The reinventers counter that it is the "low politics" of administrative routine that has handicapped governance in the United States, and that this routine must be transformed if government is to work better.

The most valuable contribution of the reinventers is their frank recognition that the top-down bureaucratic authority approach guiding American bureaucracy since the Progressive era no longer effectively steers public management. The traditional approach is not obsolete; it can never be so long as the United States is a government of laws. But it must be adapted to a new reality of shared responsibility for common purposes. Boundary spanning coupled with customer service offer fresh insights to attacking new and inescapable administrative realities. Traditional bureaucratic theorists face the challenge of fitting old notions of neat hierarchical control to an increasingly messy administrative state where bureaucratic boundaries are the beginning, not the end, of the management process.

The reinventing government movement, however, too quickly brushes away the internal inconsistencies within its own theory. Three threads of the reinventing fabric — downsizing, reengineering, and continuous improvement — compete to define it. There is, moreover, little consensus on what "customers" really means or how to serve them. The movement also too easily dances across critical but unsolved issues. Reinventing government depends on resolving difficult political and technical problems in performance management. And, even if these are resolved, customer service, competition, and performance measurement combined can never really substitute for top-down accountability. That leaves the reinventers with the difficult puzzle of adapting the valuable pieces of their own movement with the driving forces of constitutional bureaucracy.

The problem of reinventing government really revolves around these issues: Just what *do* we expect government to do? How can the bureaucratic power required to do the job well be held accountable to elected officials and, in the end, to the people? In sorting through these problems, historian Garry Wills writes, "We have been eating into our intellectual as well as our financial capital."[146] We need to stop eating our seed corn and begin anew to build the capacity to solve these problems.

Neither the traditional administration theorists nor the reinventers have full answers to the problems. New administrative realities have overtaken traditional theory, while tough and often undiagnosed problems plague the reinventing movement. Furthermore, their debate surfaces, in a new way, the ageless question of how to balance energy in the executive with checks on potential abuses of executive power. If Hamilton, Madison, and their followers could not resolve them, there is little chance that either side will find an answer that sticks.

Nevertheless, even if reinventing government raises more questions than it answers, they are the right questions. Furthermore, they are not questions likely to go away, for the administrative issues are fundamental and the political stakes are high. One of the best-kept secrets of the NPR, in fact, was that many of its quickest successes emerged from initiatives begun in the Bush administration. In fact, Republican efforts to redefine that party's soul have notable similarities with both *Reinventing Government* and the NPR.[147] The genie is out of the bottle. The struggle now is for who will control it. The basic issues are both ageless and well understood. The struggle revolves around which values, especially executive power and legislative control, will shape the administrative process.

History teaches us two important lessons about that struggle. It is unlikely to be resolved to everyone's satisfaction at any moment or to anyone's satisfaction over time. On the other hand, periodic shifts — from the Progressive movement through the New Deal, from the Great Society through the Reagan administration's downsizing — have produced huge changes in both policymaking and implementation. The reinventing government movement marks one of those important historical shifts in how we work out these questions. It is neither the fad that its critics condemn nor the fountainhead of reform that its proponents contend. It is, however, a fresh opportunity to rethink the system under which we govern ourselves: to update old ideas to fit new problems, to experiment with fresh policy solutions for enduring dilemmas, to rethink the government capacity required to solve problems, to inject new energy into the effort, and to reshape the social contract between civic responsibility and governmental power.

The NPR's strategy of launching a revolution without prescribing its form was a brilliant masterpiece. It allowed a breakout from the dominant ideas: that the size of the federal government could not be reduced; and that federal bureaucrats were stuck in existing behavior and could not be moved. The NPR produced enormous enthusiasm for change, especially because of its fuzziness. By promising bureaucrats more power and citizens a smaller and more effective government, the NPR was able to gather many good ideas under the same broad tent. Under the tent, however, the ideas of the revolution crowded uneasily with each other.

In the short term, that was of little moment. The NPR, in six very hectic months in the middle of 1993, produced an enormous contribution in jump-starting the bureaucracy. In the long term, however, these problems threaten to be the NPR's undoing.

The single biggest problem with the NPR was that, while it had a strategy leading to the release of its report on September 7, 1993, it had no strategy for September 8 and afterward. The NPR staff played a cheerleader role, to coordinate a handful of crosscutting issues like procurement reform and customer service, and to leave the other management reforms to executives across the government. What they did not do was to create an explicit strategy for linking the two revolutions, or for inducing cynical or busy executives to join in the small-politics battles.

As a result, downsizing became the dominant theme and driving reality. The tactics of reinvention had the strongest effect where they fit the preexisting strategies of managers, especially cabinet secretaries. They had little effect where managers did not see their utility in reaching larger ends. In those agencies, the NPR had little leverage and scant success in creating incentives to lure busy, reluctant or frightened executives into the revolution. In fact, it is a misnomer to speak of *the* NPR. "The NPR" was little more than the accumulation of individual actions by administrators throughout the federal government.

Any management reform, of course, has meaning only to the extent that managers throughout an agency adopt it. With the NPR, however, the problem was that it developed no mechanism for converting the unwashed or the reluctant. Many managers throughout government understandably replied that they had seen it all before. Downsizing the federal bureaucracy only increased their cynicism.[148] Many managers said that they saw little empowerment or reinvention, but they certainly felt the reality of a shrinking work force and the pressures of doing more work with less help.

Without now building a much stronger foundation, the NPR risks leaving behind a worse reality than the one from which it started. Government could be smaller, but the number of layers and regulations could be little changed. The quality of management could diminish even further. Worse yet, having raised expectations to great levels, the pain that continued performance problems will surely produce could even further diminish public trust and confidence in government. And, should that occur, even the victory of producing a smaller government will be Pyrrhic, for voters and government managers alike.

This dismal picture need not occur. In *A Christmas Carol*, Ebenezer Scrooge was given the gift of seeing the ghost of an unpleasant yule yet to come and the opportunity to prevent it from happening. The NPR has the same opportunity.

Taking advantage of that opportunity has to begin with a revolution in thinking about federal management. Every important federal management reform of the last generation has been derivative of innovations at either the state and local level, the private sector, or sometimes foreign governments. Elected officials, seeking new leverage over the bureaucracy or fresh ideas with which to appeal to voters, have culled the "greatest hits" of other organizations. In particular, they have tended to extract the most attractive little-politics ideas to promote big-politics aims. They have adopted only broad themes without learning the music, so the songs never come out quite the way they were written. They have taken music written for other ensembles and grafted it onto the federal government, which often has neither had the instruments to play it well nor the mission to perform that kind of music. And by borrowing so heavily on music written elsewhere, they have undercut the federal government's own ability to fashion the tunes that fit its own orchestra best.

Nowhere is this problem more obvious than in the enthusiasm to downsize. The federal government's downsizing movement derives heavily from private sector initiatives of the late 1980s and early 1990s. It has the obvious additional appeal to voters who are convinced they receive little value from the federal government. The private sector, however, is already beginning to learn painful lessons from its own downsizing experiences; the federal government is on the verge of stumbling into the movement's worse problems. In analyzing private sector downsizing programs, management expert Peter Drucker argued forcefully, "We are seeing way too many amputations before the diagnosis."[149]

Research is now beginning to mount that the initial advantages of corporate downsizing have often produced higher long-run costs.[150] Stressed workers burn out, leave, or remain with lower morale. Large cuts in staff tend to "penalize departments that are slim and reward those that are oversized," management analyst Eileen Applebaum concludes. The biggest performance differences, in fact, appeared due more to the quality of management than strategic downsizing (or upsizing).[151] Indeed, a study of 531 American corporations by the Wyatt Company revealed private sector downsizing rarely helped companies achieve the goals of higher profits and lower costs. Moreover, employee morale and motivation among surviving employees suffered. More successful efforts, on the other hand, began from a clear vision for the future coupled with a fundamental restructuring of the organization, from top managers to front-line employees. In fact, the biggest private sector successes came when people came to see change as an ongoing process instead of a short-term event.[152] These findings lead to five important lessons for the reinventing government movement.

1. Successful reinvention requires coupling the driving ideas of the movement to the federal government's mission. Private management reforms teach an important but little understood lesson: reforms derived from some organizations and applied blindly to others typically create more mischief than success. Any successful reform has to be tailored closely to the fundamental mission and management problems of the organization. The NPR gathered together ideas about reform from any source it could find, and it used them to start the revolution.

Many of these ideas are disconnected from what the federal government does and how it does it, however, and they provide weak guidance to harried government managers. For example, no one can quarrel with the customer service program's goal of making government services more responsive. But as now framed, it is a weak guide for action. Simply charging managers to develop customer service programs without thinking carefully about what that means in the federal system will surely mean painfully re-learning the most important lesson of private management reform: powerful ideas plucked out of context and grafted onto the wrong kind of stock will never take.[153]

Making reinvention work requires creative thinking about how to do the federal government's work better. Borrowing ideas from other organizations is a start but it is not enough. The federal government cannot simply consume knowledge about management practice. It must get far more strongly in the business of developing new knowledge. Careful thinking about management must be encouraged throughout the bureaucracy. More important, such thinking, powered by an in-depth understanding of what the federal bureaucracy is and what it does, must be the driving mission of high officials close to the president: in OMB, OPM, and the White House staff itself. "Too often we end up reengineering trains that don't connect," one observant state government official said.[154]

2. Successful reinvention requires linking the big-politics of downsizing with the small-politics of performance improvement. The biggest temptation in reinventing government is to reach for quick success by embracing downsizing without doing the hard work of improving performance; or to seek performance improvement while resisting the powerful political movement driving a reduction in the size of government. The single most important reality of American public management for the coming decade is the need to solve the inescapable paradox that the two movements present. Big-politics downsizers will have to reckon with the fact that, without careful planning, they could dumbsize the federal government, worsen performance, and even further enrage voters. Little-politics performance improvers will have to reckon with the fact that expectations will increase as resources shrink. Unlike previous management reforms, the pressures that produced the reinventing movement show no sign of evaporating.

Making reinvention work requires a frank recognition that neither piece of reinvention can proceed without the other — and that, to date, the movement has been singularly unsuccessful in charting a course to do that. The pieces sit uneasily next to each other within the NPR report, and in the agencies they have proceeded even more uneasily. The continued work of reinventing government requires a frank recognition among all parties about the tensions that its principal elements create, that the tensions cannot be escaped, and that charting a course through them will challenge the very best of our public managers.

The missing link in the NPR's effort to bridge the gap is attention to the number, position, and role of political appointees. It is inconceivable that government could be invented, that managers could be empowered, that programs could achieve results, if the political appointees who direct government agencies are not part of the plan. It is also inconceivable that the number of layers could be reduced without dealing with what Paul Light has perceptively described as the "thickening" problem.[155] Nowhere in government is the layering problem worse than at the top, in the rarefied atmosphere inhabited by political appointees. Careful attention to their role has to be part of any real effort to reinvent government.

3. Successful reinvention requires developing a language for talking about it. Just as the reinventers have not yet reconciled the conflicting elements driving their reforms, they have not yet discovered an effective way of talking about their work. Part of the problem came from short-term tactics to appeal to the public through the mass media. The vice president broke ash trays and laughed about rules preventing buying floor wax off the shelf. Indeed, these symbols represented deep-seated problems that had to be solved, and they did attract media attention to the typically dull problems of public management. However, these symbols celebrated the revolution without encouraging government workers to join in. Here, yet again, were public officials making fun of their best efforts to negotiate through an unforgiving system; in most cases, they did not make up such nonsensical rules for their own amusement but wrote them to fit the dictates of Congress and political appointees. The effort to build public support often undercut the NPR's ability to recruit government workers to the movement.

Making reinvention work requires reinventing the media and citizenship. As leaders, government officials have a responsibility to educate and shape public discourse instead of simply feeding its worst preconceptions. Many of the most publicized symbols of the NPR, like the ash trays and piles of regulations, have outlived their usefulness. NPR officials now need to develop a second generation of symbols to communicate what the work of reinvention requires and what it produces. Counting the number of executive orders issued or the number of NPR recommendations on which work has started will simply not be enough. Reinventing government depends on building a new partnership between elected officials and the government's managers, and between government and its citizens. The new symbols will have to communicate the shared responsibility that these partnerships require. The Clinton administration has made an important start, in initiatives like food stamp "smart cards" and effective disaster relief for California earthquake victims, but the broader message has not yet begun to sink through. If the administration allows its new initiatives to be judged on the terms of past failures, the reinventing government movement will surely wither.

4. Successful reinvention requires reinventing the job of federal managers, especially in government's middle. The most important, if the most quiet, failure of the early months of the NPR's implementation of its report was the widespread alienation of middle managers from the movement. The downsizing galloped far ahead of the strategy that was to drive it, and the spread of the NPR's empowerment initiatives proved wildly uneven. Their reaction was scarcely surprising; they heard the talk about new partnerships but saw the overriding reality of personnel cuts amidst rising expectations.

To a degree that many cabinet secretaries, let alone top White House and congressional officials, fail to realize, middle managers shape the work of government. Top officials can make policy and set priorities, but those priorities take hold only if the managers responsible for meeting them produce results. It is quite another thing to build partnerships with union officials and pass out permission slips to lower-level workers, but the partnerships and permission slips will work only if supervisors create an environment that promotes them.

The reinvention movement must far more effectively connect its stirring rhetoric with its strategic and tactical planning. Managers on the front lines have come away from meetings with some NPR officials convinced that they simply did not understand what managers in the field had to do to make programs work.[156] NPR officials could reshape their rhetorical flourishes and better connect with the mangers they are trying to motivate if they moved their headquarters out of Washington, or at least established an important field office beyond the Beltway, where the real work of reinvention is happening. "The NPR is as isolated as any other government agency," one government official said.[157]

More important, if the reinventers are serious, they must move from the bold rhetoric to the hard work of changing the systems. Unless they do, federal managers will be left with new demands, a smaller work force, obsolete management systems, higher expectations, and lower morale. Foremost is the need to reshape the personnel system: to produce new job categories that reflect what future managers will have to do and to create the incentives for attracting the best people to do them; to allow managers more flexibility in deploying and rewarding their staffs; to allow managers greater versatility in matching the personnel system to the needs of their agencies; and to allow supervisors greater authority to hire the best, fire the worst, and reward the most hard working employees. Civil service reform was a constant subtext of the NPR report, but it since has slipped into a black hole of inaction. Without fundamental reform of the civil service, the federal government will never be able to match its employees with the new jobs they must do or to attract the best employees to do those jobs.

5. Successful reinvention requires creating the glue to bind the movement together. The NPR has operated under the assumption that, once launched, the movement would become self-directed. Federal managers, newly empowered, would exert their energy to manage more effectively. The history of management reform, however, demonstrates that managers are rightly skeptical of big changes introduced in their interest. Faced with a choice of taking large risks toward uncertain ends or riding out the storm in an admittedly leaky boat, many managers choose to take the conservative course. On the other hand, some managers who take bold steps will surely walk in a direction different from the one that either their supervisors or members of Congress will support. Reining in the overeager or misdirected, without eliminating incentives for bold action, is a huge challenge for the movement.

OMB's reorganization, to support its more fundamental look at larger performance issues, is an important source of glue to hold the movement together and focus its attention more sharply. To the degree to which OMB can combine budgetary and management perspectives, input measures with outcome results, short-term budget marks with long-term performance, it will fundamentally alter the discourse about what matters in the federal government. The task is a large one, but to a degree that even NPR officials might not appreciate, the OMB effort is central to gluing together the two revolutions of reinvention.

Holding the revolution together ultimately will depend on how Congress reacts to it. The single biggest omission in the NPR was a strategy for dealing with Congress. The report seemed to suggest that its logic would be irresistible to members of Congress; that public support for its recommendations would make it impossible for members of Congress to disagree; or that the big picture supplied by the reinventing government movement would help Congress escape more parochial perspectives. The first months of the NPR proved the folly of an implementation strategy that did not include Congress. The struggles over the buyout bill, followed by House rejection of downsizing within VA hospitals and opposition to privatization of the air traffic control system, demonstrated that congressional support (or at least the absence of strong opposition) is critical to everything the NPR wants to accomplish. For a movement founded on building partnerships, the absence of a strategy for building a partnership with Congress was surprising. Success in the NPR will surely require quick attention to constructing that partnership.

Even more fundamentally, achieving the NPR's promise will require more clearly linking the question of *what* government ought to do and *how* government ought to do it. The NPR, in the report's own words, "focused primarily on *how* government should work, not on *what* it should do."[158] The burden of a century of public management research, however, is that the distinction is artificial: the how powerfully shapes the what because means embody ends; and, from the beginning, the how has to be driven by the what.[159]

To a greater degree than even political noncombatants stop to recognize, and certainly far more than government officials ever acknowledge, many public performance problems are often the product of what government sets out to do. Government in fact does many things very well, from delivering social security checks to providing weather satellite maps. Often, when things work badly, it is because it tries to do things that are very hard or impossible, like preventing drug abuse, training unemployed workers, cleaning up toxic waste, or providing welfare without creating dependence.

Improving performance on one level requires focusing government most clearly on the things it does well and figuring out how to do them better. However, we (and this includes the NPR, policymakers, and Americans in general) have not thought clearly about what those things are. On another level, if we seek to do things that are hard to do well, we must be frank about the degree of difficulty and focus sharply on how to do the impossible better. Many of the most basic questions to which the NPR has addressed itself revolve around such issues. If we choose to attack these problems at a superficial level, by focusing on the number of bureaucrats that can be eliminated or the dollars that can be saved, we will both miss the real issues and even further undercut government's ability to perform well.

The National Performance Review accomplished, in just its first year, far more than anyone thought possible. It energized employees, it attracted citizens, it drew media attention to government management, and it made the point that management matters. In the blush of success, however, the NPR failed to build the foundation for success in the long haul. It borrowed bits and pieces of management reform from both the public and private sectors and pasted them together in a patchwork that, while initially attractive, could not hold together. In the process, the NPR missed the most important lesson that other successful reforms teach: in the long run, management, matched to mission, matters most. The movement launched in September 1993, however promising, was not self-sustaining. Making it stick requires hard work on tough questions — work that, for the most part, has not begun.

Notes

1. "National Performance Review" has taken on three different meanings: the six-month survey of federal management, conducted by hundreds of federal managers during the middle of 1993; the report that survey produced, <u>From Red Tape to Results: Creating a Government That Works Better and Costs Less</u> (Report of the National Performance Review, September 7, 1993); and the effort that followed to put the report's recommendations into effect. I will follow the convention and use "NPR" to refer to all of these pieces of the NPR. The meaning will be clear from the context.

2. Before the waivers, OMB required that all government forms, including surveys, be cleared prior to use. The result frequently was a months-long delay before surveys could be used, which prevented government officials from gaining timely information about citizens' views.

3. At the time this report was written, Senate and House conferees were meeting to reconcile different versions of the legislation.

4. <u>From Red Tape to Results</u>, p. 89.

5. The passage of the 'buyout' bill in March 1994, which is discussed below.

6. According to the NPR's electronic network, "A Reinvention Lab is a place that cuts through 'red tape,' exceeds customer expectations, and unleashes innovations for improvement from its employees. Depending on the priorities of an agency, a lab may focus upon programs, processes, administrative structures, or a combination of all three. A lab provides a focus for reinvention efforts, diminishes the fear of failure that accompanies risk, and provides opportunities to highlight the successes of reinvention and to recognize the people responsible for those successes."

7. National Performance Review, <u>Reinvention Roundtable</u> (May 6, 1994), pp. 1, 3.

8. Interview with Public Health Service officials, May 18, 1994.

9. See, for example, Eliza Newlin Carney, "Still Trying to Reinvent Government," <u>National Journal</u>, June 18, 1994, pp. 1442-44.

10. R. Kent Weaver explores these traps in "Reinventing Government or Rearranging the Deck Chairs? The Politics of Institutional Reform in the United States," paper

prepared for the Fulbright Symposium on Public Sector Reform, Brisbane, Australia, June 23-24, 1994.

11. David Osborne and Ted Gaebler, <u>Reinventing Government: How the Entrepreneurial Spirit Is Transforming the Public Sector, from Schoolhouse to Statehouse, City Hall to the Pentagon</u> (Addison-Wesley, 1992), p. 25.

12. For a broader view of the history of administrative reform, see Gerald J. Garvey's chapter in John J. DiIulio, Jr. and Donald F. Kettl, eds., <u>Inside the Reinvention Machine: Appraising Governmental Reform</u>, (Brookings, forthcoming 1994).

13. This, in fact, was the basis of our argument that management reform depends far more on evolution than invention. See John J. DiIulio, Jr., Gerald Garvey, and Donald F. Kettl, <u>Improving Government Performance: An Owner's Manual</u> (Brookings, 1993), pp. 1-3.

14. The count comes from the General Accounting Office, <u>Management Reform: GAO's Comments on the National Performance Review's Recommendations</u>, GAO/OCG-91-1 (December 1993), p. 1.

15. National Performance Review, "Reinventing Government: Six Month Status Report" (photocopied, March 7, 1994).

16. <u>From Red Tape to Results</u>, pp. iii-iv.

17. H.R. 3400, "The Government Reform and Savings Act of 1993."

18. The work force reduction calculations were complex. When he first took office, Bill Clinton promised to reduce federal civilian employment by 100,000 workers. The NPR increased the number by 152,000, for a total of 252,000, and used the number of employees at the beginning of fiscal year 1993 as the baseline. When Congress acted in March 1994 on the bill to make the reductions possible, it used the actual fiscal year 1993 employment level, which produced a baseline 20,900 higher than the NPR figure. That resulted in a target for the downsizing of 272,900 employees.

19. Quoted in Tom Shoop, "Targeting Middle Managers," <u>Government Executive</u>, vol. 26 (January 1994), pp. 11-12.

20. Ibid., p. 13.

21. For an analysis of the buyout, see Tom Shoop, "Exodus," <u>Government Executive</u>, vol. 26 (June 1994), pp. 43-47.

22. Quoted in Shoop, "Targeting Middle Managers," p. 12.

23. Letter, CBO Director Robert D. Reischauer to Rep. Richard A. Gephardt, November 15, 1993; and Steven Greenhouse, "Budget Office Disputes Savings in Gore's Plan," New York Times, November 17, 1993, p. A13.

24. Administration officials estimated that regular turnover alone would not be enough to hit the target. They calculated, therefore, that they would have to offer inducements for federal employees to take early retirement and devised a $25,000 one-time payment for employees who resigned or retired early.

25. For a history of administrative reform, see Gerald Garvey's chapter in Inside the Reinvention Machine.

26. Interview with the author.

27. Interview with the author.

28. See Beryl Radin's chapter in Inside the Reinvention Machine for descriptions of how different departments and agencies managed the task.

29. Charles H. Levine with Rosslyn S. Kleeman, "The Quiet Crisis of the Civil Service: The Federal Personnel System at the Crossroads" (Washington: National Academy of Public Administration, December 1986). An updated version of this classic paper appears in Patricia W. Ingraham and Donald F. Kettl, Agenda for Excellence: Public Service in America (Chatham House Publishers, 1992), pp. 208-73. The quotation comes from the updated version, p. 208.

30. National Commission on the Public Service (Paul A. Volcker, Chairman), Leadership for America: Rebuilding the Public Service (Lexington Books, 1989), p. 4. See also Mark L. Goldstein, America's Hollow Government: How Washington Has Failed the People (Business One Irwin, 1992).

31. From Red Tape to Results, pp. 87-88.

32. Ibid., p. 87.

33. National Partnership Council: A New Vision for Labor-Management Relations (Draft Report to the President on Implementing Recommendations of the National Performance Review, January 1994), p. iii.

34. Stephen Barr, "OPM Turns Over 10,000 New Leaves," Washington Post, January 28, 1994, p. A21.

35. Stephen Barr, "Adieu, SF-171," Washington Post, May 9, 1994, p. A1.

36. For a description, see Tom Shoop, "Swing Your Partner," Government Executive, vol. 26 (March 1994), p. 34.

37. See National Performance Review, Reinventing Human Resource Management (GPO, September 1993), p. 93. Recommendation HRM05.1 said: "Reduce by half the time required to terminate federal managers and employees for cause. Make other improvements in the systems for dealing with poor performers."

38. OPM runs the Federal Executive Institute in Charlottesville, Virginia, as a training center for senior career civil servants about to enter the Senior Executive Service (SES). The Senior Executives Association represents members of the SES.

39. Quoted in Shoop, "Swing Your Partner," p. 33.

40. Allan J. Kam and G. Jerry Shaw, "Managers and Top Professionals Band Together," The Public Manager (Winter 1993-94), p. 8. The article also contains a history of the development of the Coalition for Effective Change.

41. Coalition for Effective Change, "Comments on NPC Report: Create a Flexible and Responsive Hiring System" (photocopied, March 1, 1994), pp. 3-4.

42. Office of Personnel Management, Union Recognition in the Federal Government (December 1992), part I, p. 2.

43. Ibid., part I, pp. 1-2.

44. FedNews (National Association of Government Employees), January 1994, p. 1.

45. Government Training News, vol. 17 (November 1993), p. 1.

46. Government Executive, vol. 26 (July 1994), p. 6.

47. Interview with the author, June 3, 1994.

48. Quoted in Shoop, "Targeting Middle Managers," p. 13.

49. "Gore on the Future of the Federal Executive," Government Executive, vol. 26 (May 1994), p. 54.

50. Interviews with the author. See also James E. Colvard, "In Defense of Middle Management," Government Executive, vol. 26 (May 1994), pp. 57-58.

51. Levine with Kleeman, "The Quiet Crisis in the American Public Service," in Ingraham and Kettl, Agenda for Excellence, pp. 261-63.

52. An important step in this direction is an accompanying report to the NPR's, Reinventing Human Resources Management.

53. The NPR explored some of these issues in greater depth. See Creating Quality Leadership and Management (GPO, September 1993).

54. For a much more extensive and extremely thoughtful analysis of the problem, see National Academy of Public Administration, Leading People in Change: Empowerment, Commitment, Accountability (Washington: National Academy of Public Administration, 1993).

55. Denis Ives, "After Managerialism: The Emerging APS [Australian Public Service]," paper prepared for the Fulbright Symposium on Public Sector Reform, Brisbane, Australia, June 23-24, 1994, p. 9.

56. For example, the Federal Quality Institute has assembled a draft "basic training" guide for those who conduct such exercises throughout the federal work force. See Creating a Customer-Driven Government (Federal Quality Institute, draft, 1994).

57. Public Service Commission, A Framework for Human Resource Management in the Australian Public Service (Canberra: Public Service Commission, 1992), p. 73.

58. Derived from Office of Personnel Management, Human Resource Development in the Federal Service: Fiscal Year 1991 (GPO, 1993), p. 2.

59. Interviews with the author.

60. For one very useful view, see Paul Light, "Do We Still Need an OPM?" Government Executive, vol. 26 (March 1994), p. 51.

61. National Performance Review, Office of Personnel Management (GPO, September 1993), p. 1.

62. Thomas J. Peters and Robert H. Waterman, Jr., In Search of Excellence: Lessons from America's Best-Run Companies (Harper & Row, 1982).

63. See Peter F. Drucker, Innovation and Entrepreneurship: Practice and Principles (Harper and Row, 1985).

64. See the transcript of the discussions that Vice President Gore held with business leaders, government officials, and academics in Philadelphia. National Performance Review, Reinventing Government Summit (photocopied, June 25, 1993).

65. For just two examples, see first the exchange in Governing between H. George Frederickson, "Painting Bull's Eyes Around Bullet Holes" (October 1992), p. 13; and David Osborne, "The Power of Outdated Ideas" (December 1992), p. 61. Then see the exchange in Government Executive between Ronald C. Moe, "Let's Rediscover Government, Not Reinvent It" (June 1993), pp. 46-48, 60; and David Osborne, "Reinvention Revisited" (July 1993), p. 56. See also David Rosenbloom, "Have an Administrative Rx? Don't Forget the Politics," Public Administration Review, vol. 53 (November/December 1994), pp. 503-07.

66. Federalist Number 70.

66. Federalist Number 70.

67. For an excellent history, see Francis E. Rourke, "Whose Bureaucracy Is This, Anyway? Congress, the President and Public Administration," <u>PS: Political Science and Politics</u>, vol. 26 (December 1993), pp. 687-92. See also Laurence E. Lynn, Jr., "Government Lite," <u>The American Prospect</u> (Winter 1994), p. 138.

68. Critics like Moe and Rosenbloom, in particular, were Madisonians who quickly criticized the concentration of executive power that the NPR advocated.

69. Harold Seidman and Robert Gilmour, <u>Politics, Position, and Power: From the Positive to the Regulatory State</u>, 4th ed. (New York: Oxford University Press, 1986).

70. See Ronald C. Moe, "The 'Reinventing Government' Exercise: Misinterpreting the Problem, Misjudging the Consequences," <u>Public Administration Review</u>, vol. 54 (March/April 1994), pp. 111-22.

71. In DiIulio, Garvey and Kettl, <u>Improving Government Performance</u>, we explained the importance of these theories in management reform. See pp. 24-28.

72. See, for example, R.H. Coase, "The Nature of the Firm," <u>Economica</u>, vol. 4 (November 1937), pp. 386-405; Armen A. Alchian and Harold Demsetz, "Production, Information Cost, and Economic Organizations," <u>American Economic Review</u>, vol. 20 (1972), pp. 777-95; Michael Jensen and William Meckling, "Theory of the Firm: Managerial Behavior, Agency Costs, and Ownership Structure," <u>Journal of Financial Economics</u>, vol. 3 (October 1976), pp. 305-60; and Terry Moe, "The New Economics of Organization," <u>American Journal of Political Science</u>, vol. 20 (1984), pp. 739-75. Excellent analyses of the theory are Charles Perrow, <u>Complex Organizations: A Critical Essay</u>, 3rd ed. (Random House, 1986), chap. 7; Gary J. Miller, <u>Managerial Dilemmas: The Political Economy of Hierarchy</u> (Cambridge University Press, 1992); and Gerald Garvey, <u>Facing the Bureaucracy: Living and Dying in a Public Agency</u> (Jossey-Bass, 1993)

73. The leading student of transaction costs is Oliver Williamson. See <u>The Economic Institutions of Capitalism</u> (Free Press, 1985).

74. Jonathan Boston, "Origins and Destinations: New Zealand's Model of Public Management and the International Transfer of Ideas," paper prepared for the Fulbright Symposium on Public Sector Reform, Brisbane, Australia, June 23-24, 1994; and Jonathan Boston, John Martin, June Pallot, and Pat Walsh, eds., <u>Reshaping the State: New Zealand's Bureaucratic Revolution</u> (Oxford University Press, 1991).

75. Interview with the author.

78. Ronald C. Moe, Edward Davis, Frederick Pauls, and Harold Relyea, "Analysis of the Budget and Management Proposals in the Report of the National Performance Review" (Washington: Congressional Research Service, photocopied, September 21, 1993), p. 4.

79. Ronald C. Moe, "Let's Rediscover Government, Not Reinvent It," Government Executive, vol. 25 (June 1993), p. 47.

80. Moe, "The 'Reinventing Government' Exercise," p. 131.

81. In Improving Government Performance: An Owner's Manual (Brookings, 1993), we also recommended reduction in middle management, but as part of a broader strategy for rethinking supervision and information in the federal government. For another view, see Tom Shoop, "Targeting Middle Managers," Government Executive, vol. 26 (January 1994), pp. 10-15.

82. Frederickson, "Painting Bull's Eyes Around Bullet Holes."

83. Moe, "The 'Reinventing Government' Exercise," p. 131.

84. Frederickson, "Painting Bull's Eyes Around Bullet Holes."

85. Moe, "The 'Reinventing Government' Exercise," p. 132.

86. Lynn, "Government Lite," pp. 141, 143.

87. Osborne and Gaebler, Reinventing Government, pp. 76-80.

88. In the forthcoming Inside the Reinvention Machine, I explore these theoretical issues and disputes in more detail.

89. Among many sources, see Christopher Hood and Michael Jackson, Administrative Argument (Aldershot, England: Dartmouth, 1991); Christopher Pollitt, Managerialism and the Public Services: The Anglo-American Experience (Basil Blackwell, 1990); Jenny Potter, "Consumerism and the Public Sector: How Well Does the Coat Fit?" Public Administration, vol. 66 (Summer 1988), pp. 149-64; Robin Hambelton, "Consumerism, Decentralization and Local Democracy," Public Administration, vol. 66 (Summer 1988), pp. 125-47; John Stewart and Kieron Walsh, "Change in the Management of Public Services," Public Administration, vol. 70 (Winter 1992), pp. 499-518; Task Force on Management Improvement, The Australian Public Service Reformed: An Evaluation of a Decade of Management Reform (Canberra: Australian Government Publishing Service, 1992); State Services Commission, New Zealand's Reformed State Sector (Wellington: State Services Commission, 1994). For a survey of management reform in industrialized nations, see Organization for Economic Cooperation and Development, Public Management Developments: Survey 1993 (Paris: OECD, 1993).

90. See William A. Niskanen, Jr., Bureaucracy and Representative Government (Aldine-Atherton, 1971); Allan H. Meltzer and Scott F. Richard, "Why Government Grows (and Grows) in a Democracy," The Public Interest, no. 52 (Summer 1978), pp. 111-18; and E. S. Savas, Privatization: The Key to Better Government (Chatham House Publishers, 1987).

91. Donald F. Kettl, Sharing Power: Public Governance and Private Markets (Brookings, 1993).

92. The General Accounting Office struggled, with only modest success, to define what an "inherently governmental function" is. See Government Contractors: Are Service Contractors Performing Inherently Governmental Functions? GGD-92-11 (November 1991).

93. See Osborne and Gaebler, Reinventing Government, esp. chaps. 3 and 7; and From Red Tape to Results, pp. 62-64.

94. Leonard D. White, Introduction to the Study of Public Administration (Macmillan, 1950), p. 8. Emphasis in original.

95. See Marver H. Bernstein, The Job of the Federal Executive (Brookings, 1958).

96. See Frederick C. Mosher, Democracy and the Public Service, 2d ed. (New York: Oxford University Press, 1982).

97. On the last point, see Charles O. Jones, The Presidency in a Separated System (Brookings, 1994).

98. Interview with the author, July 7, 1994.

99. Michael Hammer and James Champy, Reengineering the Corporation: A Manifesto for Business Revolution (New York: HarperBusiness, 1993), p. 17.

100. A different approach to management reform, continuous improvement, reaches similar conclusions about the importance of customers. See, for example, Peter M. Senge, The Fifth Discipline: The Art and Practice of the Learning Organization (Doubleday, 1990).

101. See Graham T. Allison, "Public and Private Management: Are They Alike in All Unimportant Respects?" Proceedings for the Public Management Research Conference (November 19-20, 1979); Office of Personnel Management, Document 127-53-1 (February 1980), pp. 27-38. Allison, in turn, built on Paul Appleby, Big Democracy (Alfred A. Knopf, 1945).

102. From Red Tape to Results, p. 44. Emphasis in original.

103. National Performance Review, Improving Customer Service (GPO, September 1993).

104. Improving Customer Service, p. 5. For a discussion, see Tom Shoop, "From Citizens to Customers," Government Executive, vol. 26 (May 1994), pp. 27-30.

105. General Accounting Office, Veterans Benefits: Status of Claims Processing Initiative in VA's New York Regional Office, HEHS-94-183BR (June 17, 1994).

106. Frederickson, "Painting Bull's Eyes Around Bullet Holes."

107. We expanded on the argument that follows in Improving Government Performance, pp. 48-54.

108. The Clinton administration decided to reintroduce the wolves against the strenuous objections of the ranchers. See Dirk Johnson, "Yellowstone Will Shelter Wolves Again," New York Times, June 17, 1994, p. A6.

109. Donald F. Kettl, Government by Proxy: (Mis?)Managing Federal Programs (Washington: Congressional Quarterly Press, 1988).

110. For a sweeping examination of these problems, see American Society for Public Administration, Improving Management and Performance in the Federal-State-Local System (Recommendations of the Symposium on Public Administration, photocopied, September 1993).

111. The Oregon Option: A Proposed Model for Results-Driven Intergovernmental Service Delivery (photocopied, July 25, 1994).

112. Oregon Progress Board, Oregon Benchmarks: Standards for Measuring Statewide Progress and Government Performance (Salem: Oregon Progress Board, December 1992). See also Neil R. Peirce, "Marking Progress Oregon-Style," The Oregonian, April 11, 1994, p. B7.

113. The Oregon Option, p. 18.

114. George Frederickson, "George and the Case of the Government Reinventors," PA Times, vol. 17 (January 1, 1994), p. 9.

115. See Jonathan Rauch, Demosclerosis: The Silent Killer of American Government (Times Books, 1994).

116. See Robin Hamilton, "Consumerism, Decentralization and Local Democracy," Public Administration, vol. 66 (Summer 1988), pp. 125-47; Jenny Potter, "Consumerism and the Public Sector: How Well Does the Coat Fit?" Public Administration, vol. 66 (Summer 1988), pp. 149-64; Mary Seneviratne and Sarah Cracknell, "Consumer

Complaints in Public Sector Services," <u>Public Administration</u>, vol. 66 (Summer 1988), pp. 181-93; John Stewart and Kieron Walsh, "Change in the Management of Public Services," <u>Public Administration</u>, vol. 70 (Winter 1992), pp. 499-518; and Peter Aucoin, "Administrative Reform in Public Management: Paradigms, Principles, Paradoxes and Pendulums," <u>Governance</u>, vol. 3 (April 1990), pp. 115-37.

117. A public good is one in which an individual's consumption of it does not diminish another individual's ability to consume.

118. Potter, "Consumerism and the Public Sector," p. 159.

119. See Donald F. Kettl, "Deregulating at the Boundaries of Government: Would It Help?" in John J. DiIulio, Jr., ed., <u>Deregulating the Public Service: Can Government Be Improved?</u> (Brookings, 1994), esp. pp. 178-79.

120. Panetta later became President Clinton's chief of staff, and Rivlin replaced Panetta as OMB director.

121. Statutory management responsibilities would continue to remain under the supervision of separate offices: the Office of Federal Management, the Office of Federal Procurement Policy, and the Office of Information and Regulatory Affairs.

122. Office of Management and Budget, Office Memorandum No. 94-16 (March 1, 1994).

123. Ibid.

124. See Alan Dean, Dwight Ink, and Harold Seidman, "OMB's 'M': Fading Away," <u>Government Executive</u>, vol. 26 (June 1994), pp. 62-64.

125. OMB Director Leon Panetta, who issued the order launching the OMB 2000 reorganization, ironically had introduced a bill while chairman of the House Budget Committee to create a separate office of federal management.

126. Public Law 103-62, Sec. 2(b)(1).

127. Office of Management and Budget, "Evaluation Framework for Assessing Implementation of GPRA" (photocopied, February 1, 1994); and interview, August 3, 1994.

128. See the 1994 revision of Circular A-11.

129. For a review of the issues, see several General Accounting Office reports: <u>Performance Measurement: An Important Tool in Managing Results</u>, GAO/GGD-92-35 (May 5, 1992); <u>Program Performance Measures: Federal Agency Collection and Use of Performance Data</u>, GAO/GGD-92-65 (May 1992); and <u>Performance Budgeting: State Experiences and Implications for the Federal Government</u>, GAO/AFMD-93-41 (February

1993). See also Joseph S. Wholey, Evaluation and Effective Public Management (Little, Brown, 1983); James E. Swiss, Public Management Systems: Monitoring and Managing Government Performance (Prentice-Hall, 1991); Congressional Budget Office, Using Performance Measures in the Federal Budget Process (July 1993); and John J. DiIulio, Jr., and others, Performance Measures for the Criminal Justice System (Government Printing Office, 1993).

130. See CBO, Using Performance Measures in the Federal Budget Process; and Performance Budgeting: State Experiences and Implications for the Federal Government. For a discussion of both methods and background issues, see Swiss, Public Management Systems.

131. CBO, Using Performance Measures in the Federal Budget Process, p. xiii.

132. A very useful approach to understanding these distinctions is Robert N. Anthony and David W. Young, Management Control in Nonprofit Organizations, 5th ed. (Irwin, 1994).

133. Matthew D. McCubbins and Thomas Schwartz, "Congressional Oversight Overlooked: Police Patrols Versus Fire Alarms," American Journal of Political Science, vol. 28 (Fall 1984), pp. 169, 172.

134. From Red Tape to Results, esp. pp. 110-19.

135. For a careful analysis of the NPR's congressional strategy, see Christopher Foreman's chapter in the forthcoming Inside the Reinvention Machine.

136. Christina Del Valle, "The Job-Training Squabbles: Is This Any Way to Reinvent Government?" Business Week, August 1, 1994, p. 37.

137. See Carney, "Still Trying to Reinvent Government," p. 1444, for an analysis of the critical role of congressional support in following through on the NPR.

138. See Budget of the United States Government, Analytical Perspectives, Fiscal Year 1994 (GPO, 1994), pp. 275-98; and General Accounting Office, Improving Government Performance: Actions Needed to Sustain and Enhance Management Reforms, GAO /T-OCG-94-1 (January 27, 1994).

139. GAO, Improving Government Performance, pp. 26-27.

140. See Kettl, Sharing Power, for an analysis.

141. See U.S. House of Representatives, Committee on Government Operations, Managing the Federal Government: A Decade of Decline, majority staff report (GPO, 1992); and Committee on the Budget, Management Reform: A Top Priority for the Federal Executive Branch, committee print, 102 Cong. 1 sess (1991).

142. For case studies, see Kettl, <u>Sharing Power</u>.

143. Vice President Gore did, however, emphasize the importance of learning in a speech, "Overcoming Cynicism about Change in the Federal Government," remarks prepared for the Seventh Annual National Conference on Federal Quality, July 13, 1994.

144. Paul Holley, "Pilot Program at Local VA Is 'Reinventing' Government," <u>The [Milwaukee] Business Journal</u>, April 23, 1994, p. 2.

145. On "low" versus "high" politics, see Charles T. Goodsell, "Did NPR Reinvent Government Reform?" <u>The Public Manager</u> (Fall 1993), pp. 7-10.

146. Garry Wills, "Can Clinton Close the Vision Gap?" <u>New York Times</u>, November 8, 1992, sec. 4, p. 17.

147. See, for example, James P. Pinkerton, "General Schwarzkopf's New Paradigm," <u>Policy Review</u>, No. 56 (Summer 1991), pp. 22-26; and "Life in Bush Hell," <u>The New Republic</u> Vol. 207, No. 25 (December 14, 1992), pp. 22-27.

148. Gore's speech, "Overcoming Cynicism about Change in the Federal Government," identified cynicism as a major challenge to government reform.

149. Quoted by Frederick Rose, "Job-Cutting Medicine Fails to Remedy Productivity Ills at Many Companies," <u>Wall Street Journal</u>, June 7, 1994, p. A2.

150. Peter Scott-Morgan, <u>The Unwritten Rules of the Game</u> (McGraw Hill, 1994).

151. Rose, "Job-cutting Medicine Fails to Remedy Productivity Ills at Many Companies," pp. A2, A16. See also Rosalind Klein Berlin, "Burned Out Bosses," <u>Fortune</u>, July 25, 1994, pp.44-52.

152. <u>Best Practices in Restructuring: Wyatt's 1993 Survey of Corporate Restructuring</u> (Washington: The Wyatt Company, 1993), pp. 9, 11, and 43.

153. See Tom Shoop, "From Citizens to Customers," <u>Government Executive</u>, vol. 26 (May 1994), pp. 27-30.

154. Interview with the author.

155. Paul Light, <u>Thickening Government: Federal Hierarchy and the Diffusion of Accountability</u>, (Brookings, forthcoming).

156. Interview with the author.

157. Interview with the author.

158. <u>From Red Tape to Results</u>, p. ii.

159. A very useful comparison of how ideas and practice collide is James Q. Wilson, "Mr. Clinton, Meet Mr. Gore," <u>Wall Street Journal</u>, October 28, 1993, p.A22.

Appendix I

The Draft Australian Competency In "Client Service"

1   Interact with clients
      1.1   Receive enquiries
            1.1.1   Enquiry is acknowledged and action to respond initiated promptly/without delay
            1.1.2   Access and equity issues are considered

      1.2   Process applications/claims
            1.2.1   Application or claim is processed promptly
            1.2.2   Enquiry is processed in accordance with established process and/or current standing instructions
            1.2.3   Irregularities are resolved

      1.3   Provide advice
            1.3.1   Advice provided assists clients to reach decisions or take informed action
            1.3.2   Advice is timely and appropriate to the clients' needs
            1.3.3   Response is timely, polite, and helpful

      1.4   Establish client needs
            1.4.1   Clients' requirements are met
            1.4.2   Post service feedback is obtained

2   Market/promote the service
      2.1   Conduct research in the market
            2.1.1   Client needs are identified and understood
            2.1.2   Market trends are identified and strategies recommended to accommodate changes
            2.1.3   Service standards are adjusted to meet changed needs
            2.1.4   Regular feedback from clients and the market place is received

2.2 Promote the service(s) to clients
    2.2.1 Clients use the services offered
    2.2.2 Clients are aware of and understand the nature and standard of services on offer

2.3 Ensure clients have access to the service(s) on offer
    2.3.1 Client disabilities are considered in the design of documentation accompanying services
    2.3.2 Alternative methods of delivery are available wherever appropriate
    2.3.3 Promotion material is available and reflects accurately on services on offer and process(es) to be followed by the client

3 Evaluate service delivery
   3.1 Monitor service delivery
       3.1.1 Agency standards are maintained and quality service is provided
       3.1.2 Statistical information is collected and collated accurately
       3.1.3 Records are maintained in accordance with established policy and procedure
       3.1.4 Reports clearly indicate the level of performance achieved and any action required to adjust or rectify procedures
       3.1.5 Access and equity principles are addressed and maintained

   3.2 Review procedures
       3.2.1 Procedures are reviewed on a regular basis to ensure currency
       3.2.2 Outcomes satisfy specifications

   3.3 Determine client satisfaction with service and delivery
       3.3.1 Client input is actively sought to gauge levels of satisfaction
       3.3.2 Client service feedback is recorded and reported

   3.4 Survey clients, prospective clients, and the market environment
       3.4.1 Clients' needs are identified and understood
       3.4.2 Service or product standards satisfy client/market needs
       3.4.3 Service/product changes reflect changes in the service environment
       3.4.4 Clients' comments are addressed

   3.5 Establish client contacts
       3.5.1 Client contacts are appropriate
       3.5.2 Contacts readily respond to enquiries

   3.6 Analyze survey results
       3.6.1 Survey results are recorded and analyzed
       3.6.2 Changing trends are identified and reported
       3.6.3 Recommendations for action or new services are provided

4   Manage service/product delivery
    4.1   Plan service operations to meet client needs
        4.1.1   Service(s) offered satisfy client needs
        4.1.2   Operations are adjusted to changing client requirements

    4.2   Consult with staff and unions on operational practices and proposed improvements
        4.2.1   Staff and unions are involved in planning or alteration of practices
        4.2.2   Staff and union views are taken into account when change is being considered

    4.3   Negotiate with clients on services and standards
        4.3.1   Client views on services and standards are regularly addressed
        4.3.2   Changes are discussed with clients prior to implementation

    4.4   Provide appropriate service(s)
        4.4.1   The service(s) satisfies the recognized/established need
        4.4.2   Client service standards are satisfied within resource constraints and completing priorities
        4.4.3   Client complaints are reduced

Source: Australian Public Service Commission, "Joint APS Training Council Meeting" (Agenda, 28-29 June 1994).

About the Brookings Center for Public Management

The Brookings Institution's new Center for Public Management was founded in January 1994. The advisory council to the Center is chaired by Paul A. Volcker, former chairman of the Federal Reserve System, and former chairman of the National Commission on the Public Service. The Center is led by John J. DiIulio, Jr., Professor of Politics and Public Affairs at Princeton University, and Nonresident Senior Fellow at Brookings. The Center is part of the Brookings Governmental Studies program.

The Center is dedicated to improving the public service and the processes by which democratically-enacted public policies are implemented. The Center supports three main sets of activities: (1) the design, execution, and timely publication of public management research on cutting-edge problems of federal, state, and local governance; (2) civic education and outreach efforts (symposia, reports, awards, op-eds) intended to keep policymakers, public administrators, journalists, and others informed about the crucial public management dimensions of public policy and governance; and (3) leadership and management training programs for selected government executives and managers.

In July 1993, Brookings published Improving Government Performance: An Owner's Manual, the first major independent analysis of the Clinton administration's "reinventing government" initiative, the National Performance Review. Last January Brookings released Deregulating the Public Service: Can Government Be Improved?, a critical study of the key assumptions behind many federal, state, and local bureaucracy reform initiatives. Several other volumes are forthcoming this year from the new Brookings center, including *Making Health Reform Work: A View From the States* and *Inside the Reinvention Machine: Appraising Governmental Reform*. Other Center projects include an analysis of the administrative consequences of divided party government, a study of public sector performance measurement and budgeting, and an effort to assist the federal government in administering the community policing provisions of the pending crime bill. The Center's core leadership and staff are:

Leadership: Paul Volcker, Former Chairman, Board of Governors, Federal Reserve System; Thomas E. Mann, Director, Governmental Studies, The Brookings Institution; John J. DiIulio, Jr., Professor of Politics and Public Affairs, Princeton University, Director, Brookings Center for Public Management; Donald F. Kettl, Professor, La Follette Institute of Public Affairs, University of Wisconsin - Madison, Visiting Fellow, Brookings Institution; Gerald J. Garvey, Professor of Politics, Princeton University; Christopher H. Foreman, Senior Fellow, Brookings Institution; and Constance Horner, Former Director, Federal Office of Personnel Management, Guest Scholar, Brookings Institution.

Staff: Carey Macdonald, Brookings Institution; and Cindy Terrels, Brookings Institution.